The Temp Track

Make One

of the Hottest Job Trends
of the 90s
Work for You

Peggy O'Connell Justice

Peterson's
Princeton, New Jersey

Library of Congress Cataloging-in-Publication Data
Justice, Peggy O'Connell, 1948–
    The temp track : make one of the hottest job trends of the 90s work for you / Peggy O'Connell Justice.
       p. cm.
Includes index.
ISBN 1-56079-254-X : $12.95
    1. Temporary employment. 2. Temporary employees. I. Title.
HD5854.J87 1993
331.25'72—dc20   93-5877
                                                  CIP

Text design by CDS Design

Composition by Peterson's Guides

Printed in U.S.A.

10 9 8 7 6 5 4 3 2

Dedication

To Marilyn N. O'Connell, my mother, for her unceasing support and unusual perspective on life, and to the people I consider family: my friends and my direct, step, former, late, and future relatives. Thank you all for the support and laughs.

Also in memory of Toby O'Connell, Lelia and Ed Mitchell, and Fannie Maki Nelson.

Contents

Acknowledgments

My sincere thanks to the many people in the temporary help service industry—temps, coordinators, and client company representatives—I've spoken to and met over the years. Although I may not have mentioned you by name, your input is here.

Special thanks to the following people and companies whose contributions directly or indirectly helped make this book possible:

Nanda Scott

Jane Coviello

Lisa Noe, R.N.

Thomas Parnham

Mark Stevenson, R.N.

Bruce Steinberg, National Association of Temporary Services

Susan Minzter, Cooperative Concepts

Theresa Daly, *Staffing Industry Report*

David A. Lord, *Executive Recruiter News*

Mike Kutka, *Tempdigest*

Sandra Pesmen, Crain Communications Inc.

John Chuang, MacTemps

James Fromstein, Manpower Inc.

Nancy Mallahan, Routhier Placement Specialists

Tom Routhier, Routhier Placement Specialists
Betty Brittingham, Claim Net
Deb Hester, Chameleon Creatives, Inc.
Pat Brie, J. R. Personnel/Aid Temporary
Pat McDonough, Office Specialists
Janeen Checketts, CompHealth/Kron
David Hermann, EDD of Florida, Inc.
Janet Christopher, Advance Personnel Associates Inc.
Rae Plante, Advance Personnel Associates Inc.
Donald Truss, Science Temps
Zack Mark, Science Temps
Judith Serio, Lawstaf, Inc.
Bob Lyons, Olsten Technical Services
Rick Kehoe, TAD Technical Services
Heather Patay, Talent Resources Company, Inc.
John LaRosa, Marketdata Enterprises, Inc.
John Riley, Transworld Services Group

In particular, I'd like to acknowledge and thank Carol Hupping, executive editor at Peterson's, for her expert guidance and support.

Introduction

If you've been following the national media, you have most likely heard that American business has been restructuring and using temporary workers to help them do it. Many companies have discovered that they can save big money by operating with only a core of full-time workers who are assisted, as needed, by contingent workers and are hiring temps in great numbers.

Using temps on such a large scale has been called the most important trend in business today—one that will fundamentally change the relationship between Americans and their jobs.

Temps who now make more money and work fewer hours than they did as full-time workers will rave about the pluses of temp work. Those who have been laid off and are working in lesser capacities as temps will naturally give you a negative opinion. Whether the boom in temporary workers in American business is a positive or a negative trend is, of course, important and the subject of much debate, but debating the pros and cons of it wouldn't be of much help to you. Positive, practical advice on using temporary work to its fullest advantage may be, as you'll see.

The information you'll find between the covers of this book has been gathered from experts in the field, temporary workers themselves, and my own wide range of experience as a temp in professional and clerical fields over the course of ten years. I don't pretend they or I have solutions to any problems posed by temporary work, nor do I wish to minimize the drawbacks in emphasizing the pluses. Although it can be great for millions of people in many circumstances, temping is not, as I'll stress, for everyone.

But much of what I've found out about temporary work in the 90s is good news for people who want to earn money as they're building up their resume, job hunting, learning new skills, and gaining a variety of work experiences. A savvy temp can thrive in today's new business world. Read on and I'll tell you how.

Get On the Temp Track

If you're looking for work, a good job, or flexibility and challenge in your working life, you've come to the right book.

No matter what your job skills, level of experience, age, gender, education, or circumstances, temping can mean money in your pocket today, a better job outlook for tomorrow, and a chance to take charge of your career.

Now, I know most of us have read so many sweeping statements like the one I just made that we don't pay attention to them anymore. You may think it sounds unrealistic to say temporary work can help *anyone* find work or better work no matter who they are. But it's true.

If you have a tough time believing that, maybe it's because your ideas about temporary workers are out of date. If you still think temps are secretaries who fill in when full-time secretaries go on vacation, it's time to revise your definition. Drastically.

Today's temporary workers are men and women of all ages who work in nearly every conceivable field. Again, this is not just another meaningless statement. I really mean *all ages* and *nearly every field there is*.

Engineers, nurses, draftsmen, writers, editors, accountants, bank officers, biochemists, assembly-line workers, security guards, managers, executives, computer programmers, medical technicians of all types, pharmacists, radiologists, salespeople, scientists, lawyers, flight attendants, doctors, pilots, high school principals, paralegals, human resources directors, beauticians, and CAD/CAM designers are all working on a temporary basis today—and that's just a sampling of occupations.

As Michael R. Losey, president and CEO of the Society for Human Resource Management, puts it, "Temporary workers in the 1990s possess an astounding variety of skills. While clerical and secretarial workers continue to be a staple for the market, employers can also pick up the telephone and ask for a CPA, civil engineer, registered nurse, operations manager, financial analyst, or even a CEO."[1]

Every day over a million people work as temps in over a million different places for over a million different reasons. They may not always be referred to as temps: You may also hear terms such as contract workers, per diem workers, locum tenens personnel, line consultants, jobbers or job shoppers, flexible executives, executive temps, extra workers, short-timers, or peripherals. In England, where the executive temporary work market alone is a $175- to $260-million-a-year industry, the term independent consultancy is sometimes used to refer to executives who work on a temporary basis. Essentially, all the terms mean the same thing—temporary workers.

Why are all these people working as temps? There are several good reasons.

TEMPING CAN GET YOU WHAT YOU WANT

Savvy temps can reach a variety of goals by taking an entrepreneurial approach and making the most of temp work. You can use temporary work to:

- get inside companies where the unadvertised jobs are
- try out jobs and fields before making a commitment

- back up a great part-time or seasonal job you couldn't otherwise afford to take
- gain work experience in a variety of jobs
- make job contacts
- network in the most effective way possible
- expand your resume
- gain and round out practical skills
- jump onto the middle of the corporate ladder instead of starting at the bottom
- learn firsthand what "cutting edge" companies are doing in your field
- choose when and where you want to work while pursing avocations and dreams, raising children, or going to school
- break out of the nine-to-five grind and choose from a wide variety of jobs you'll actually enjoy
- work for and learn from leaders in your field

Of course, there are pitfalls as well as opportunities in temping, and I do have to address the problems, especially now that business is using the temporary help service industry as a restructuring tool to get "lean and mean." I will, but first things first. Before I get into the details, I'll give you a quick overview of what temp work is all about and bring out some important points to keep in mind.

TEMPS ARE NOT JUST SECRETARIES ANYMORE

Temporary workers have been with us since the turn of the century. However, the temporary help industry as we know it today really became established during the time of World War II, when there was a huge labor shortage and women were often needed to fill vacancies left by men fighting overseas. (Men were secretaries before women took over, don't forget.) These first temps, nattily dressed in white gloves and charming hats, often filled clerical positions and came and went as the workload demanded. The arrangement worked so well that millions of women have held positions as temporary secretaries and office workers ever since.

Although men and women in countless other fields have gradually joined these temporary clerical workers, the image of secretaries remains so strong that, to this day, many people don't realize that temps can be a whole lot more than clerical workers. Sometimes today's temporary workers don't even recognize themselves.

WHO ARE THE TEMPS OF TODAY?

Only a few years ago, that would have been an easy question to answer, but not anymore. Look at the following examples and see if you think these people are temps:

- A friend's wife, Jane, is a nurse anesthesiologist. Rather than work at one general hospital and stand idly by waiting for whatever routine operations come along in the course of a day, she prefers to work in her area of expertise, open-heart surgery. To make this possible, she works through a locum tenens company that places her in hospitals that routinely schedule open-heart surgery procedures. (Locum tenens is the special term used for health personnel who work on a temporary basis.) Usually one hospital keeps her busy, but when other hospitals have more than the usual number of operations scheduled, they call on Jane and other medical personnel who work for Jane's company. Would you call Jane a temp? She certainly wouldn't call herself one.

- Tom, who loves his freedom so much he routinely refuses full-time job offers (even though his temp assignments have him working full time), designs print circuit boards for high-tech companies. His assignments are arranged by what he calls a contract servicing company, which also pays his weekly salary. Is he a temp? No, he says, he's a job shopper. Sometimes he works for the same company for years, he argues.

- And what about my nurse friend, Karen? For the past

four years she has worked in hospitals across the country (and once in Saudi Arabia) through what she calls a medical recruiter. During Mardi Gras she worked in a New Orleans hospital; during ski season she was in Colorado. Is Karen a temp? She calls herself a traveling nurse.

Their assignments may be much longer than what used to be typical, may require advanced degrees, and may be arranged by a company that does not call itself a temporary help company. But still, all of these people are not employees of the client companies they work for, and they are not part-timers or freelancers. So what else could they be but temporary workers?

WHAT'S IN A NAME?

The terminology used in the temporary service industry is clearly inadequate. As it stands, the term temp includes physicians saving lives as well as 16-year-old high school students lumping fish crates. In an attempt to categorize different levels of temporary workers, I've heard people use the term elite temps for doctors, lawyers, and scientists, executive temps for high-level business people, and professional temps for all highly skilled and educated temps.

These, too, are inadequate terms. Clerical temps are also professionals, after all, and it's a myth that they're not educated. Even before the explosion in the number of "professionals" working as temps, 82 percent of all temps had more than a high school education, 47 percent had some college or business school education, and 35 percent had college degrees, according to a 1989 survey by the National Association of Temporary Services (NATS), a trade association that represents approximately 85 percent of the temporary help industry.[2] So much for stereotypes. And who would have the nerve to call himself or herself an elite temp?

To say someone is a temp, meaning temporary worker, is the

same as calling a full-time employee a full—it doesn't say nearly enough. Temp what? Full what?

For now, though, temp is the term we have to work with. For lack of a better definition, when I use the word temp in this book I'll be talking about anyone who is sent to work at one company, medical facility, or work site but is paid by another company that has arranged the assignment.

TEMP HELP COMPANIES

Just as there are a variety of terms for temps, there are also a number of names for what are essentially temporary help companies. You may hear a nurse use the term service, agency, or per diem contractor, while a CAD/CAM operator may refer to a placement specialist or job shop company.

Different fields use different terms. Some companies don't even attempt to define themselves with terms and simply assume that people in the business are aware of the service they provide. Sometimes you have to ask around in your industry and study help-wanted ads to find appropriate companies.

TYPES OF COMPANIES

There are specialized temp companies that place people exclusively in science, medical, accounting, or legal fields, for example, and others that provide a full range of workers, from receptionists to senior executives. Some specialized and "niche" companies are experts in providing one very specific type of skilled worker, such as senior insurance adjusters, while others concentrate on the mainstay of the industry, which is still clerical and light industrial workers of all kinds.

Altogether, the temporary service industry today is a nearly $25-billion-a-year business, and it's growing. The world's biggest temp help company, Manpower Inc., has a pool of 560,000 people to send out on assignments, and there are well over 5,000 other temp help companies in the U.S., many with offices throughout the country and the world.

THE FAST-CHANGING TEMP INDUSTRY

Depending on your age and experience, you may already be aware of some of the information I'm about to present. You may even think that some of what I tell you goes without saying. But since the range in age and experience of people who could benefit from temporary work is so great, I cannot assume that everyone has the same knowledge on the subject. Also, keep in mind that the temporary employment field is evolving so rapidly that it's impossible to keep up with news on the subject. Don't be surprised if you know of some new developments in the industry that I don't mention in this book.

As I write this, some temporary help companies are:

- staying open for business 24 hours a day
- developing specialized divisions
- offering full benefits, including 401(k) plans
- training data entry temps using individual client companies' own forms before they're sent to an assignment
- running on-site, in-house temporary pools for major employers
- becoming computerized for easier skill matching
- offering extensive, industry-specific training
- signing long-term service agreements with state agencies or private companies
- putting star temps on their full-time payroll to avoid losing them to other temp help companies

LENGTH OF ASSIGNMENT

How long an assignment lasts tends to vary depending on the field of work and type of assignment. Traveling medical personnel, for example, are often expected to commit for three months, while an engineer may work until a project is over, which could be a year or

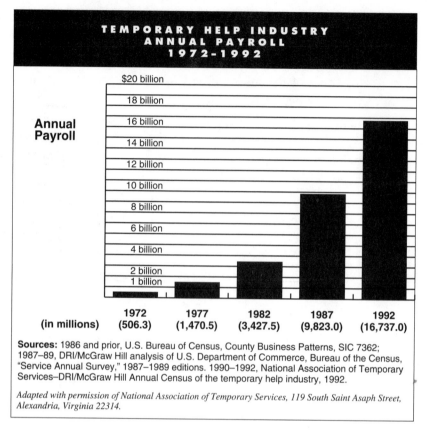

TEMPORARY HELP INDUSTRY ANNUAL PAYROLL 1972-1992

Annual Payroll

	$20 billion
	18 billion
	16 billion
	14 billion
	12 billion
	10 billion
	8 billion
	6 billion
	4 billion
	2 billion
	1 billion

	1972	1977	1982	1987	1992
(in millions)	(506.3)	(1,470.5)	(3,427.5)	(9,823.0)	(16,737.0)

Sources: 1986 and prior, U.S. Bureau of Census, County Business Patterns, SIC 7362; 1987–89, DRI/McGraw Hill analysis of U.S. Department of Commerce, Bureau of the Census, "Service Annual Survey," 1987–1989 editions. 1990–1992, National Association of Temporary Services–DRI/McGraw Hill Annual Census of the temporary help industry, 1992.

Adapted with permission of National Association of Temporary Services, 119 South Saint Asaph Street, Alexandria, Virginia 22314.

more. Clerical and light industrial temps may be needed for a half-day's work or indefinitely.

PAY SCALE

As you can imagine, when temps can be anyone from teens with no work experience to the proverbial rocket scientist, the pay range is great. Salaries start at minimum wage for unskilled workers and can climb to $600-plus a day for top-level managers.

What you can make as a temp depends on a number of factors that you'll have to identify before you start. As a general rule, though, Samuel R. Sacco, executive vice president of NATS, says that most positions available through temporary help companies offer an hourly pay scale that is equal to or higher than the same hourly rate paid to a permanent employee in the same position.

There are, of course, exceptions to this rule. So-called elite

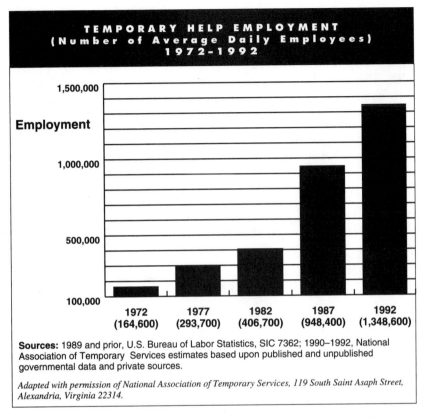

TEMPORARY HELP EMPLOYMENT
(Number of Average Daily Employees)
1972-1992

Employment				
1972	1977	1982	1987	1992
(164,600)	(293,700)	(406,700)	(948,400)	(1,348,600)

Sources: 1989 and prior, U.S. Bureau of Labor Statistics, SIC 7362; 1990–1992, National Association of Temporary Services estimates based upon published and unpublished governmental data and private sources.

Adapted with permission of National Association of Temporary Services, 119 South Saint Asaph Street, Alexandria, Virginia 22314.

temps, for example, have been known to make twice the best salary paid to their full-time equivalents, depending on how much in demand their skills are. In an overcrowded field the rates could be lower than the standard.

MIXING GENERAL AND PROFESSIONAL TEMPING

You've probably been hearing a lot about new "professional" temp jobs, which perhaps has given you the impression that there's a lot of work for highly skilled temps. Well, yes and no. The amount of work available in professional fields varies from region to region and from field to field. In general it's about 25 percent of the total temp work force.

If you have specialized, advanced skills in a booming field, you may find all the work you need through one temporary help company specializing in temps with your skills. But if you don't, and you need a paycheck, you may have to supplement your "professional" assignments with more traditional or general skilled temporary assignments. This may not be all bad. In fact, it could have advantages.

Besides providing opportunities to pick up practical, marketable skills, general skilled assignments can get professionals inside companies they might otherwise have only dreamed of entering with specialized skills. As you'll see in the following chapters, many people have landed great jobs this way.

THE BIGGEST DRAWBACKS OF TEMPING

In general, but not always, the two main problems with temp work are the lack of job security and adequate benefits. I don't wish to minimize these problems; I know they can keep people awake at night worrying, because as a temp I've worried myself about these same issues. But consider the following:

- How much job security do full-time employees really have?

  Many people who are temping today say they have more job security now than they did when working full time. As savvy temps out in the working world, they're picking up more experience, exposure, contacts, and job offers than they did when they were stuck in a dead-end job—where, during a time of "lean and mean" restructuring, they never felt safe from the ax.

- Better benefits for temps may be on the horizon.

  You may have heard that temps receive no benefits. This is not entirely accurate and requires investigation on your part. Many temporary help companies have always offered basic benefits to temps who have worked for them exclusively for a predetermined period. Some companies, especially those that place highly skilled temps, offer fantastic benefits and bonuses you'd never find on an equivalent full-time job. I discuss benefits in chapter 7. For now, keep in mind that you haven't yet heard the whole story on this subject.

continued on page 14

THE TRADITIONAL PROS AND CONS OF TEMPORARY WORK

Pros

The temporary service industry has grown steadily since World War II because it continues to provide:

- an incomparably effective way to shop around for and land a full-time job
- opportunities for on-the-job experience and training
- a convenient way to earn money while in transition (retiring, between jobs, relocating, changing fields, etc.)
- a well-established way to enjoy a flexible schedule

Cons

The main drawbacks of the industry as a whole *traditionally* have been:

- lack of job security
- few or no benefits and privileges, such as health insurance and retirement, vacation, and holiday pay
- possible down time between assignments
- possible image problems

I stress the word "traditionally" in listing the cons because the temporary service industry today is huge, and it's undergoing an amazing transformation. All the old truths are changing. In some fields, depending on skill level, none of these negative aspects of temporary work still apply. Some temps get better than full benefits, more work than they can handle, better money than they could earn as full-time employees, and a high level of respect.

On the other end of the scale, there are people now working as temps who make far less than they used to as full-time employees. It's not at all uncommon to hear of CEOs working as accountants on short-term assignments for a fraction of their former salary and suffering a major hit to their self-esteem. It's also true that unskilled workers are finding it tough to compete for assignments, let alone enjoy all the pluses temporary work has to offer.

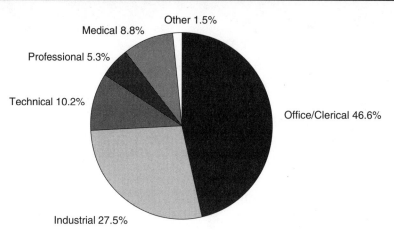

Office/Clerical includes secretaries, general office clerks, filing clerks, receptionists, typists, word processor operators, data entry keyers, telemarketers, cashiers, product demonstrators, etc.

Industrial is the blue collar segment and includes manufacturing personnel, factory workers, shipping and receiving clerks, etc.

Technical includes computer programmers, computer systems analysts, designers, drafters, editors, engineers, and illustrators.

Professional includes accountants, auditors, CFOs, paralegals, attorneys, sales and marketing personnel, as well as those in middle and senior management.

Medical includes supplemental staffing to hospitals, nursing homes, outpatient clinics, etc. and home health care with both licensed RNs, LPNs, trained medical personnel, and unlicensed home health aides, homemakers, etc.

Sources: National Association of Temporary Services (NATS)–DRI/McGraw Hill Annual Census of the temporary help industry conducted exclusively for NATS, 1992.

Adapted with permission of National Association of Temporary Services, 119 South Saint Asaph Street, Alexandria, Virginia 22314.

****

I'll talk in more detail about all these points as we go along, but for now I can tell you that I think you're going to be amazed when you realize how versatile and diversified temporary work is today—and what it can do for you.

Now let's look at how you can fit into the picture.

CHAPTER 2

What Temping Can Do for You

To make a go of temping, you can't just sign up with a temporary help company and then wait for your phone to ring. Essentially, you have to be a marketer. You have to promote your skills, hustle after the best assignments, negotiate your fees, work the phones, manage your schedule, cultivate relationships with people who can help you, and position yourself to move up in your career.

It takes some work, but it's work that can pay off in ways you may never have imagined. Here are some examples.

HELP YOU FIND A FULL-TIME JOB

You can send out literally hundreds of resumes in response to ads in the newspaper and still not get a job. Why?

Because hundreds of other people in your field with similar backgrounds are doing the same thing. Chances are, the person who is going to get the job is someone the employer already knows. As you no doubt realize by now, networking—finding a job through word of mouth—works.

In fact, networking is a lot more effective than answering classified ads, sending out unsolicited resumes, or just about anything else. But why network when you can walk into any number of companies, get right to work, meet everyone in the place, and get paid while you're doing it?

Consider the possibilities. What would you think if many of the people at the company where you wanted to work, including the human resources director, department head, and perhaps even the president, knew you, liked you, and thought you did a great job? You'd think you had an in, wouldn't you? Well, you would.

It's only human nature to stick with what we're sure of. Why would an employer hire a stranger based on a resume (usually overinflated) and one or two interviews when he or she knows another candidate (you) who has done a great job and is liked by everyone in the company?

True, there is no guarantee that as a temp you'll get assignments at the companies you'd like to work for or that the jobs will even be in your field, but you'll certainly have opportunities to network much more effectively while working for companies in your area than you would if you simply called casual acquaintances in hopes that they'd heard of a job.

TEMPING TIP

If you're offered a job at a company where you've worked before through a temporary help company, you must be sure you're not violating any contract or agreement stipulating that you won't work for a client company for a certain length of time after the temporary assignment ends. It's best to check with your temporary help company before you accept a full-time job at a company you once worked for as a temp.

TEMPING PAYS OFF IN THE LONG RUN

Two separate studies reached the same conclusion: As a direct result of temporary work, people obtain higher-paying positions.

One of the studies, conducted by Dr. Julie L. Hotchkiss of Georgia State University and released late in 1991, concluded that a person who takes a transitional (temp) job "may be better off in the long run because a transitional job will relieve enough financial pressure to give [job seekers] the bargaining power to hold out for higher wages or a better job."[3]

Another study, conducted the same year for the National Association of Temporary Services (NATS) by an independent research firm, showed that 67 percent of the respondents reported gaining new skills while they were temporary employees and 57 percent reported receiving higher wages for subsequent assignments.[4]

In 1989, 54 percent of the temporary workers polled in a third NATS survey said they had been offered full-time positions at companies where they worked as temps.[5] A lot has happened since 1989, and, depending on how the economy is doing, that percentage will rise or fall. In growing fields like biotech, the percentage of jobs offered may rise, while in low-growth fields they may dip.

The studies and surveys illustrate the point that when people are in the right place at the right time, they can find decent-paying full-time jobs if they want them. And temps are often in the right place at the right time.

EASE STRESS WHILE YOU'RE JOB HUNTING

People who have been unemployed for some time and unsuccessful in landing a job may become panicky and take the next job offered no matter what it is and what it pays, especially in tough economic times. Even if times aren't that tough, people who have lost jobs and can't find new ones start to lose confidence after a while.

When job seekers apply for a position and don't get it, the experience takes a chunk of their self-esteem until, eventually, they begin to feel unemployable. Standards and salary requirements slide lower and lower until many of them will take anything just to be working again. How often have you heard "Well, at least it's a job" in the past few years?

Temps can afford to be a whole lot pickier about jobs they accept. As Dr. Hotchkiss found in her study, people who take "transitional" jobs relieve the financial pressure enough to hold out for higher wages and a better full-time position.

In addition to easing financial difficulties, temporary work reduces the psychological pressure too. When you're working, even if it's on an assignment that requires only basic skills, you're active, productive, meeting people, and earning money—all of which can help revive shaken self-esteem. You have little time left for negative thinking and anxiety.

Sandra Pesmen, a corporate features editor for Crain Communications Inc. and a nationally syndicated columnist on the subject of jobs and careers, often advises her readers to take temporary work for a variety of reasons, even if the pay's low and the work is not in their field. "Just getting up and dressed and going off to work in the morning can boost self-esteem," she said from her home office in Chicago, "especially when people realize they're getting a foot in the door of a company and a chance to network and make job contacts. It gives people hope."

SUPPLEMENT YOUR UNEMPLOYMENT CHECKS

Should you consider temporary work if you're officially "on unemployment"? Definitely.

But before you take a temp job under these circumstances, do some research. Unemployment compensation was designed to protect people in your situation (and so many people have been in your situation!). You don't want to lose that protection; it's your safety net. That's why it's vital that you talk to the people in your state division of employment and training and your temp help company coordinator before you start temping.

You must know exactly how your claim will be affected if you take a temporary assignment. Keep in mind that unemployment regulations differ from state to state and are subject to change. Make sure, before you start, that you know what you're committing to.

TEMPING TIP

The benefits of temping while officially "on unemployment" are worth looking into if you're having trouble finding a job and think you could make the same or more by temping as you could collecting unemployment checks. If you don't work at all while collecting unemployment compensation, you could exhaust the allotment of unemployment funds you're entitled to before your claim expires. Your safety net will then be gone until you have contributed enough money to the pool through working to be eligible once again. If you work on a temporary basis, however, funds remain in your claim since your unemployment checks will be stopped or reduced while you are being paid by a temp help company. If you run out of temporary work and your claim has not yet expired, you should still have unemployment compensation coming to you. Plus, should you be laid off again from a new job, you will still have funds remaining to draw upon if you are forced to file a second claim. Best of all, while working as a temp, you are improving your chance of finding a full-time job.

TEMPING WHILE UNEMPLOYED CAN BE A PLUS

The people I spoke with at the Department of Employment and Training in Massachusetts pointed out that it is not their agency's intention to penalize people for taking temporary work. On the contrary, the agency encourages people collecting unemployment to work as temporaries for some of the same reasons I've just mentioned.

First, agency workers are aware that many people are offered full-time jobs while working as temps. Second, they know that people learn new skills on temporary assignments and can sometimes get training from temp companies, both of which can help them land a position. And third, they realize that if people are working, even as temps, there's less chance that they will fall into a depression and give up their job search.

The psychological benefits are obvious, too. Rather than stand in an unemployment line or sit at home waiting for the phone to ring, you're working. Even if you're not getting the best assignments in the world, you're getting out of the house, learning new skills, gaining confidence in your abilities, becoming more flexible, and adapting to constant change.

WHAT YOU NEED TO KNOW TO KEEP YOUR UNEMPLOYMENT COMPENSATION

Temporary work can boost your spirits—and help preserve your unemployment safety net—while you're looking for a new job. But you might unknowingly disqualify yourself from receiving future unemployment checks if you don't fully understand your state's rules and procedures about temping while unemployed. Be sure to ask the appropriate people at the unemployment office and your temporary coordinator the following questions:

- What happens to my unemployed status if I take one temporary assignment for one wage and the next week am offered only a few days' work at a low rate? Would I be considered to be refusing work if I turned it down? If so, what happens if I refuse work?
- Once I start temping, must I take every assignment that comes along? If I don't, will that be considered refusing work?
- If I'm offered a full-time job through a temporary

assignment and it's not in my field, must I take it or risk losing my unemployed status?

- Once I take work that is not in my field, must I then continue to take work assignments not in my field?
- Will my unemployment benefits be interrupted if I take a temporary assignment? If so, how? What can I expect?

If you're at all uncomfortable with the answers you receive or can't get the answers, you may want to concentrate on finding a full-time job and turn to temporary work only when you have exhausted all other options.

PUT YOUR PROFESSIONAL OR SPECIALIZED SKILLS TO WORK AGAIN

Maybe you're a retired engineer, one of too many lawyers in your area, president or vice president of a bank that went under, an executive sacrificed during corporate downsizing, a physician or scientist who wants more flexibility—in short, a highly skilled professional. If so, you may find, as many other professionals have, that temporary work can offer challenging work at a lucrative rate with a lot more flexibility than you're used to. There are temp help companies that specialize in placing skilled professionals, even professional-level executives, and you'll want to look for them. (See chapter 8 for more on specialized temping.)

Executive Recruiter News identifies 140 executive temporary placement firms in North America and Europe and estimates the U.S. market at more than $100 million. "It fits so nicely with the management ideal of a lean, mean organization and with the executive's desire for freedom, independence, and interesting work," said Richard Ball of ProTem in London.[6]

One of the reasons executive temporary help companies are successful is that they sell speed. When a permanent position opens up, a traditional executive search to fill that job usually takes three to six months, according to *Executive Recruiter News,* while executive temporary positions are filled in 5 to 15 days for jobs typically lasting three to nine months.[7]

A BIG MARKET FOR HEALTH FIELD TEMPS

Do you have skills in a medical or allied health field? Probably the most dramatic growth in recent years has been in these fields, where hospitals and health agencies are crying for temp help. "Send me 50 physical therapists," said one medical temporary help coordinator in Orlando, Florida, "and I'll place them all before I go home tonight." What's new today is the jump in demand for allied health temp workers such as phlebotomists and medical assistants.

GET A JOB, EARN MONEY AFTER GRADUATION

The frustrating adage "You can't get a job without experience, and you can't get experience without a job" doesn't apply to temporary workers. People as young as 16 find work as temporaries, and a great number of high school–age and college-age job seekers gain work experience, contacts, and opportunities for full-time employment (not to mention money) even if they're still in school.

Temping is a learning experience you just can't duplicate; it's like being an intern over and over again. You learn every day— about the business you're working in, about people, and about yourself. You can build up your resume, round out your skills, and find new job contacts if you want them, plus enjoy a flexible lifestyle—all while you're earning money.

All age groups are well represented in the temporary help service industry. A NATS survey showed that young people from 16 to 24 make up 28 percent of all temps; young adults from 25 to 34, 29 percent; adults 35 to 44, 20 percent; those 45 to 54, 35 percent, and people over 55, 19 percent.[8] These statistics may fluctuate, but the point is that you could actually work temporary jobs all your working life and even after you retire.

JOBS FOR COLLEGE GRADS

According to the Department of Education, in spring 1992, 1.1 million people graduated from four-year colleges—the largest number ever.[9] Unfortunately, the job market was the worst it had been in decades.

As a result, new college graduates flooded temporary help companies and took whatever work they could get. Admittedly, not all of the work was challenging or allowed the graduates to use their education. And even with the best schooling in the world, temporary jobs don't come automatically upon graduation. But keep in mind that there are more temp opportunities out there than ever before for everyone, experienced and inexperienced alike.

TEMP JOBS FOR WOMEN AND MEN

Traditionally it's been easier for women to use temporary work to break into fields of their choice since so many temps work as secretaries and most secretaries are women. Male temps do work in office settings, even as secretaries, but because of sexist stereotyping there are not many men willing to venture into what has become a female domain.

It used to be that 80 percent of all temporary workers were female, but as the industry expands to include many other fields besides clerical, office, and light industrial work, the statistics are changing, too. Now that there are temp lawyers, doctors, and scientists, to name just a few occupations, the ratio of male to female temps is roughly equal. It stands to reason that if the technical, professional, and medical fields are the fastest growing areas for temps, then the number of men working in those fields is increasing as well.

When I went on a job interview, long before the recession of the 1990s, I was concerned that my long list of temporary positions would not impress the personnel director as much as the long history of a full-time worker would. I was about to defend myself—by explaining that I had been working on writing projects and raising children—when she remarked on my wide range of experience and skills, all of which I had picked up as a temp. As she pointed out, I knew a lot about software languages and had worked in a number of capacities for some of the most prestigious employers in the area.

She noted my surprise and told me, "My feeling is that when I'm hiring a former temp, I'm hiring a survivor. When young people right out of college or high school come to me for a job, I tell them to go be a temp for a while. I want them to get some work experience, explore a few companies, figure out what they like and don't like about a job, learn how to deal with all sorts of people, gain skills. . . . I think temping is a tremendous education."

PROFILE OF A TYPICAL TEMPORARY EMPLOYEE

Temporary employees are well educated, value the flexibility offered by temporary employment, and have gained new skills working as temps. These were among the findings of a 1989 NATS survey of temps conducted by an independent research firm. The following profile is based on that survey.

Temporaries are well educated.

- 82% have more than a high school education.
- 47% have some college or business/trade school education.
- 35% have college degrees; 9% have graduate or professional degrees or graduate hours.

Temporaries choose temporary employment for additional income and job flexibility.

Asked to select the factors that were of importance in their decision to become temporary employees, respondents said that the following were "very" or "somewhat" important:

- Earning additional income—80%
- Working a flexible schedule—77%
- Improving skills—70%
- Having opportunities to secure full-time work—67%

Temporaries gain skills, especially computer skills.

- 67% have gained new skills.

■ 86% have gained computer skills.

Temporaries earn more as their skills increase.

■ 60% make more than $6 per hour.

■ 57% are earning more than they did in previous assignments.

Temporaries work in all regions of the country.

■ 20% work in the South.

■ 19% work in the West Central region.

■ 17% work in the East Central region.

■ 17% work in the Pacific/Mountain region.

■ 16% work in the Mid-Atlantic region.

■ 12% work in the Northeast.

The typical temporary is female and under 35 years old.

■ 80% of temps are female.

■ 29% are between 25 and 34 years old.

■ 28% are between 16 and 24.

■ 20% are between 35 and 44.

■ 13% are between 45 and 54.

■ 9% are over 55.

Other significant findings:

■ 44% provide the main source of income in their household.

■ Most have worked at least four weeks as temps.

■ 43% are married, and 80% of those who are married have spouses who are employed full time.

■ 54% have been asked to continue as full-time employees by client companies for whom they have temped.

■ 12% have retired from a full-time job.

Note: This profile is based on responses from 2,508 temporary employees who completed a confidential written questionnaire during June and July 1989. The study was conducted by Lauer, Lalley and Associates, Inc., a Washington, D.C., public opinion and market research firm.

Reprinted with permission from Contemporary Times, *Winter 1989, National Association of Temporary Services, 119 South Saint Asaph Street, Alexandria, Virginia 22314.*

GET TRAINING THAT WILL MAKE YOU MORE MARKETABLE

No one has to tell you how important education and training are today. We all know top skills are needed to compete in today's job market and that such skills need constant updating. In fact, according to NATS, 75 percent of the jobs that will exist in the year 2000 didn't exist in 1989—workers will have to be trained and retrained to do them.

As a temporary worker you can pick up job skills in two ways: through training offered by many temporary help companies and through on-the-job training at temporary assignments (although the latter is becoming less common than it used to be). See chapter 6 for more about the training you might expect to get as a temp. If you need new or updated skills, temp work is definitely something to consider.

ADVANCE IN YOUR CAREER

On a full-time job, you usually advance only when someone above you is promoted, quits, or is fired. No matter how talented you are or how hard as you work, if there isn't an opening, you generally don't move up, even though your workload may well increase.

Not so for temps. Many can advance their careers without waiting for some higher-level position to open up. Now that so many companies are operating with a drastically cut-back and over-worked full-time staff, much of the workload full-time staffers used to take on is going to temps. As a result, temps are being given opportunities that were never available before.

Rather than repeating the same type of work at the same level over and over again, temps in all fields are picking and choosing assignments, often moving in and out of full-time jobs, learning and climbing as they go.

The advantage a temp has over a full-time worker, coordinators say, is that both may have equal skills, but the full-time worker is expected to spend a year or more in a position before being considered for advancement. He or she may also be held back by supervisors who don't want to frequently retrain replacements. A temp, meanwhile, may spend mere months in increasingly advanced positions and will be encouraged to climb since higher level temps earn more money for the temp help company.

GAIN WORK EXPERIENCE

Many people today in all occupations at all levels are using temporary work to broaden their experience. "I could have made ten more dollars an hour to start if I hadn't asked my service to find me an assignment in a school system where I could work under a supervisor," said one recent college graduate who had earned a degree as an occupational therapy assistant. "I wanted to learn more, though, before I worked on my own. I have a contract for the school year, and while I'm there, I plan to pick my supervisor's brain," she told me. "There is more to this job than money. I want to be good at what I do."

In an article she wrote for *The American Journal of Nursing,* traveling nurse Paige Kester-Beaver described some of the opportunities for temps like herself: "You can work in a challenging position at a teaching facility at the forefront of technology one month and encounter an equally challenging position the next as the only registered nurse at a 20-bed hospital. The possible handicap of always being the 'new kid' is offset by the chance to practice a more focused kind of nursing."[10]

PICK UP KNOWLEDGE AS YOU MOVE FROM COMPANY TO COMPANY

Even if you have worked in your field for years, you can still gain a tremendous amount of knowledge just by "trying out" different companies or work sites. And if you don't have a long work history, you can make yourself more marketable much faster through temporary work than by staying at one job for many years.

I once worked as a temp with a very bright woman named Phyllis, who for many years had been the only support person for 14 engineers. Although the company she worked for was huge, her division was isolated from the rest of the staff in a remote spot, and she rarely came in contact with other support personnel.

Phyllis was quick and capable, yet I was stunned when I saw her separate ten copies of a five-page document into piles so she could collate them. When I pointed out that her copier had the capability to collate for her, she was embarrassed and explained that the copier was a recent hand-me-down from another division and came without a manual.

"I know I'm behind the times," she told me, "but if you don't have any instructions or a teacher, it's hard to learn. We don't use temps often, but when we do, I always learn a lot. You people move around so much, you're always up to date."

While knowing how to operate a copier is hardly an advanced skill, Phyllis made me think about how much I had learned and had taken for granted by moving from one company to another. In addition to the 14 software languages I had picked up, I had learned a lot about office equipment, methodology, and many different industries, things I never would have known had I, like Phyllis, stayed at just one company.

When you're job shopping, experience in your target industry is often a requirement. If you have such experience, as well as skills in a variety of other fields, and you can provide references from the leaders in the industry—all of which you can get through temp work—you greatly improve your chances of getting an interview.

Every company, medical facility, or work site has its own unique methods of operation and equipment, and even though the range of skills available through temporary help companies has increased, it's still difficult to find exactly the right person for the job. As a result, if you know the basics, you will be asked to apply your skills in new ways. You're always going to learn something new on each assignment you're sent to. How useful that new knowledge will be depends on the assignment. But the more assignments you take, the more skills you'll pick up. As I mentioned, I learned many different software programs through temporary work, and many temps report similar experiences in their fields, including 67 percent of NATS survey respondents who also learned new skills while on temporary assignments.

WORK DURING RETIREMENT

When we think of retiring, many of us picture ourselves at age 65, spending long, relaxing days at the beach, on the golf course, or traveling the world. But that may not be what you have in mind. Maybe you're one of those people who find that they've got too much energy and drive to enjoy total relaxation. Are you the type who would miss the daily interaction with co-workers, the feeling of accomplishment, and the sense of purpose work gives you?

If you take advantage of an early retirement option, you may have a long way to go before you're really ready to give up work entirely. And you're not alone. In fact, although there is an increase in the number of people accepting early retirement options, an American Association of Retired Persons poll revealed that Americans age 55 to 64 preferred work to retirement by a ratio of three to one.[11]

And then you may be worried about money. If you're retired, you may be finding it tough to get by on a fixed income. A part-time or a new full-time job has been the answer for some, but an increasing number of retirees are finding temporary work an even better solution.

Unlike part-time jobs, a temporary assignment keeps work challenging and interesting since you can change jobs just about whenever you want. Temporary work also can give you the flexibility in your schedule that perhaps you've been looking forward to all your working life.

Another plus is that now that the temporary help industry has expanded to include more professionals, retired people are finding more options in the kind of temporary work available, which can mean better pay and more interesting work.

GOOD OPPORTUNITIES FOR RETIREES

David Lord, managing editor of *The Executive Recruiter News,* reports, "Candidates over age 55, who may have difficulty procuring permanent positions, are, with their wealth of experience and expertise, ideal as exec temps."[12]

People retiring early (and not so early) are also finding work if they want or need it. According to NATS, older workers are now being perceived as valuable personnel resources who bring much-needed stability, wisdom, and talent to the workplace. In fact, Management Solutions, a firm in Silicon Valley, California, reported in July 1991 that about half of its 1,600 executive-level temps were over 50.[13]

TEMPING TIP

If you're retired and receiving Social Security benefits, check with your Social Security office before you start working as a temp. Your benefits won't be affected as long as your earnings don't go above a certain level, but you need to find out what that level is. Once you reach it for the year, stop accepting temporary assignments and you'll still have your benefits. It's as simple as that.

PAY FOR OLDER TEMPS

According to one temp help coordinator I interviewed, who did not want to be named in case her clients recognized themselves, some company heads believe they shouldn't have to pay retirees as much as younger people because, they rationalize, retired employees work just because they want something to do, much as a volunteer would, and not because they need the money.

Whether that's true (and it often isn't) is beside the point. People should be paid for the work they do. Some clients even have the nerve to insist on paying less to older workers because retired people have no other job options.

"This makes me furious," said one temporary help company owner. "If anything, a retired person should be paid more than a younger person because of his or her longer work experience." Rather than try to make unethical people ethical, though, some temporary help companies have made it a policy not to mention their employees' age and instead fill the assignment based on skills and leave it at that.

EARN SOME MONEY IN A HURRY

If you're out of work and need cash fast, consider temping. You could have a paycheck by the end of the week.

One great thing about a lot of temp help companies is that they pay you quickly, either the same week you work or early the next week, depending on the temp company's payroll system. Some companies even stay open late Friday nights so temps can drop by and pick up their paychecks. Companies do this because they understand that many of their employees are between jobs and need cash; they'll try to accommodate their workers by paying them as fast as they can.

TEMPING TIP

If immediate cash is what you're looking for, ask when payday is while you're shopping for temp help companies.

ENJOY A MORE FLEXIBLE WORK SCHEDULE

If anything positive can come out of a recession, with its massive number of layoffs, it is that with nothing to lose, many people at least have had the opportunity to explore other jobs and lifestyles.

"Businesses don't make lifetime commitments anymore, so employees are making some shifts too," said NATS executive vice president Samuel Sacco. One of those shifts has been to temporary work.

All across the country, temporary service coordinators are reporting an increase in the number of long-term temps. Some of these people just haven't yet found the job of their dreams, but there are others who simply do not want to make a commitment to any one company.

Pat McDonough, senior vice president of Office Specialists in Burlington, Massachusetts, said 24 percent of her temps have been temping for two years. Other companies in the area report similar figures. "We've got temps who have been working for us for ten years," said McDonough. "It's a growing trend." Her own secretary, in fact, has worked for her as a temp for nine years, despite the fact that McDonough has offered her a permanent job every six months. Her answer is "No thanks" every time. She'd rather hold on to her long summer vacations.[14]

John Riley, president of Transworld Service Group, one of Orlando, Florida's biggest and most rapidly expanding temporary help firms, pointed out in a phone interview that "the traditional 'career employee' no longer feels the company loyalty seen in the 70s and 80s and is focusing more on the quality of life. With the recent downsizing activities, many qualified individuals are entering the temporary work force and enjoying the flexibility offered by working in different environments."

During rough economic times, what have they got to lose? As one temp from Huntington Beach, California, told me, "I was offered four jobs in the last year and turned each one down. Only one of the companies that made those offers has not had major layoffs since then. Everywhere I go people walk around chanting 'at least I have a job.' I feel more secure as a temp—plus I don't have to put up with as much."

MORE FLEXIBILITY FOR PARENTS

Being a parent is a full-time job. Unfortunately, few of us have the luxury of being full-time parents these days; we have to work while we're raising a family. For a great number of people, though, temping can provide a way to make money while keeping a flexible schedule. If your children are young and you have a spouse who has a full-time job and a family health insurance plan to go with it, you might want to consider temporary work. There are a number of reasons.

If your child gets sick, you can call your temporary help coordinator and have a replacement fill in for you for the day so you can be home to dispense aspirin and TLC. Although it's trickier to arrange, you can also work "mothers' hours" and half days in the event of teacher meetings or doctor's appointments. If you can afford it, temporary work allows you to stay home when your children are on school vacation and even take summers off to be with them.

Temporary secretaries have been doing this for years, but now many professional parents have the option, too. Pam Freeman, a lawyer in New Haven, Connecticut, and the mother of two girls, eight and six, told me, "When I worked full time, I was always feeling guilty. I felt guilty that I wasn't spending enough time with my daughters and guilty that I wasn't spending enough time at the job. As a temporary lawyer, I can finish one project at a time. When the assignment's over, the project is done and I can then give my complete attention to my daughters. I don't have to endure office politics, endless hours at my desk. . . . I'm a lot happier now, and guilt-free."

EARN MORE MONEY THAN AT A PERMANENT JOB

If you're in a field that has more work than workers, or you have exceptional skills that companies need, you may make a better hourly wage or weekly salary as a temporary worker than you earned at your last job. Plus you'll gain freedom to work when and where you choose. In fact, one possible reason for the growth in the professional/technical and medical temp fields is that people with skills in these fields are finding so many high-paying assignments that they can afford to enjoy the flexible lifestyle that temporary work provides and are refusing full-time jobs when they're offered them.

FIND A JOB WHEN YOU RELOCATE

The average American moves every six years—11 times during his or her lifetime. Some of those moves are made because of new jobs. And some are made in hopes of finding greener employment pastures elsewhere.

If you're thinking about pulling up stakes and finding work elsewhere, you'll be doing yourself a big favor if you establish yourself as a temp at home before leaving for parts unknown. That way, if you're good at what you do as a temp, you'll have the confidence and know-how to find temp work much more quickly when you arrive at your destination.

Your temporary help coordinator at home may even be able to assist you if there's a branch of his or her company in the city you're headed for. In some situations, you may even be able to set up a temporary assignment before you arrive in your new city.

You could try temping for the first time when you reach your destination, but you'd be better off having a few assignments under your belt. It's stressful enough trying to adjust to a new location without having to adjust to the stress of working as a temp for the first time.

SUPPLEMENT MONEY YOU EARN FROM YOUR OWN BUSINESS

If you've built a successful business only to find your customers bailing out on you one by one because of economic hard times, consider temping on the side to keep your business solvent. Perhaps you could work at night and on weekends filling your customers' orders and work for a temporary agency during weekdays. Perhaps you could work one week for your business and the next week as a temp. Is your business seasonal? Maybe you could work as a temp during the off-season while you work for yourself during your peak season.

TEMPING TIP

If you're not in a high-growth field and don't have highly specialized skills, you may make the same money as a temp as you made in full-time work—or even less. In that case you should use temporary work only in the traditional way: as a stepping-stone in your career, which it certainly can be.

SUMMARY

Now do you begin to see the real possibilities that temping has to offer? Let me briefly review them:

- You have a better chance of landing a full-time job through temping than through many other methods.
- Most temps learn new skills.
- Temporary positions are available in nearly every field.
- Temping offers work flexibility.
- Temping gives you more control over your career.
- Temps often find opportunities for rapid advancement.
- Temping can give you an income while you're in transition.
- Temping gives you opportunities to train or retrain, often at someone else's expense.
- You can gain a great deal of experience and knowledge as a temp—while you're earning money.
- You can find work even if you're retired or a teenager, or if you have little work experience.
- Temps can make more money than, or the same money as, full-time workers.

CHAPTER 3

Are You Cut Out to Temp?

It's one thing to examine the pros and cons and possibilities of temporary work, and quite another to actually *do* it. Is temporary work really something you could do? You can't answer that question until you know all the facts that apply to your situation, and even then you won't really know until you try it. Some people are more successful as temporary workers than others simply because of personality traits. Let's look at some of those traits before we go any further. Think about these questions:

HOW FLEXIBLE ARE YOU?

You may feel strongly that there is only one correct way to perform a certain task, be it setting up a letter or going through the steps for a laboratory test, but when you're working for companies as a temporary worker, you've got to do it *their* way even if every other place you've ever worked does it *your* way. Can you accept that?

HOW CONSCIENTIOUS ARE YOU?

Would you go out of your way to help a customer over the phone even if you knew you would never hear from him or her again in your life? If you had extra time on your hands, would you voluntarily take on a task you knew needed to be done? Would you work overtime in a pinch, postpone lunch if the office needed you, or go to work early to get a job done on time even though you knew you'd be out of there for good the next day?

HOW INDUSTRIOUS ARE YOU?

The hourly rate for any type of temporary worker is relatively high since clients pay for both the temporary worker and the temp help company's service. Consequently, clients tend to envision dollars wasted if temps aren't constantly busy, even if there's nothing to do at the moment. Do you have the energy to be as productive as some clients expect?

DO YOU HAVE A SENSE OF HUMOR?

Patricia S. Fuller, who worked in New York City as a temp, recalled trying to get to one assignment: "I didn't think there could be much difference between Wall Street and Wall Street Plaza until the elevator doors opened on my appointed floor and I found myself in an empty construction site. The entire floor had been gutted back to the concrete—the wind was whistling, and I was 26 stories in the air."[15] She laughed. Would you have laughed if it had been you?

HOW RELAXED ARE YOU?

Given that you're bound to be nervous the first few times you try temporary work, how anxious are you going to be in an unfamiliar setting where you're not sure what's expected of you? Could you put up with the daily stress of dealing with new environments, the strain of emergency situations you might be called in for, the pressure of having to give the company its money's worth—plus the possibility of encountering difficult people who might feel threatened by your reputation as an expert at what you do?

HOW STRONG IS YOUR SELF-CONFIDENCE?

If you were in a high-ranking position before you became a temp, how would you feel if you found yourself totally without status in a place where no one knows you or has heard of your accomplishments?

HOW ADAPTABLE ARE YOU?

Could you work comfortably at someone else's desk, drafting table, or workstation? Would a constantly changing environment drive you crazy?

HOW FOCUSED CAN YOU BE?

On a temporary assignment, could you turn all your attention to the job at hand despite the fact that you're in a strange office where people you've never seen before are milling about, phones are ringing, and the equipment and tools you've been given are new to you?

ARE YOU A QUICK STUDY?

Do you learn quickly? Can you think on your feet?

CAN YOU WORK INDEPENDENTLY?

It's easy to say 'of course,' but when it really comes down to it, could you be left in a room with only basic instructions and figure out for yourself what is expected of you?

WHO ISN'T GOOD TEMP MATERIAL?

Practically anyone can temp—if the desire is there. Still, there are some people who simply know they aren't cut out to be temps, at least not on a long-term basis. One of them is Nancy Mallahan.

Nancy is a temporary coordinator for Routhier Placement Specialists, a company that specializes in placing temps with legal expertise in the metropolitan Boston area. Although she coordinates assignments for "legal temps" every day, she doesn't think she could be a temp herself.

"I have to give temps a lot of credit. It amazes me how adaptable and flexible they are," she said when I talked to her last. "I'm the kind of person who has to have everything just so or I'm thrown off. I like knowing my comfortable shoes are right under my desk where they always are. I function best when things are where I can find them."

Sally, an accountant I know, tried temporary work at one time but couldn't stand the lack of control she felt when she moved from office to office. "I could have made good money, but I hated it," she told me. "I'm a perfectionist. If you came into my office while I was out and sat at my desk to use the phone, I'd know you'd been there. I have to have the phone cord curled into a figure eight so it doesn't get tangled when I'm using it, and the arms of my chair have to be lined up with the corners of my blotter or the universe feels out of kilter. You should see my closet! Every hanger is evenly spaced one inch apart. There's no way I could work at someone else's desk."

Flexibility is the key to success in any type of temporary assignment. But there are varying degrees of flexibility; the range is very wide.

THE CONFIDENCE FACTOR

There is a big difference between *thinking* you can't work as a temp and *knowing* you can't. Sometimes people put up roadblocks by telling themselves they aren't cut out for temping, when the real issue is lack of confidence. Even people who have been successful at highly skilled jobs for many years can find their confidence shaken at the prospect of walking cold into a new situation.

Who among us, after all, can truthfully say they're totally confident on the first day of a new job? Lawyer, secretary, nurse, accountant, doctor, CEO—it doesn't matter who you are. Starting a new temporary assignment feels like the first day on a new job because, well, that's what it is. But that doesn't mean you can't handle it.

It's important to know that temporary work can actually help you build confidence in your abilities, no matter what your level of experience. In fact, millions of people have used temporary work to build confidence and skills before entering or reentering the work force; it's one of the most common reasons for temping.

TEMPING TIP

Probably the easiest way to build confidence as a temp is by first accepting short-term assignments you know you can do, then gradually tackling more challenging assignments. In the meantime, you're picking up work skills, experience, and self-assurance.

In more specialized temporary fields, such as nursing, an orientation period is often required, which makes adjustment to the new situation easier. Many times, though, you're expected to walk in and get right to work, and that can be nerve-racking. Can you do it? Yes, if you keep a few key points in mind.

SOME ANXIETY IS NORMAL

It's quite common for people in any field to doubt their abilities during the first day on a temporary assignment. Most temp help companies will give you a call after you've been at the job for a couple of hours to see how you're adapting. If you're overwhelmed and really can't do the job, the temp company will try to send a backup to take over.

It's in your best interest, though, to stick out an assignment if you possibly can. Unless you've proved yourself to your temp company many times over and have a really good reason why you can't do the job, it's doubtful you'll get another assignment from that company. Your temp coordinator is not going to risk your backing out of an assignment again; it's bad for business. But the most important reason to stick it out is to prove to yourself that you can survive a seemingly impossible situation, which will help build your self-confidence.

YOU CAN LEAVE IF YOU WANT

Sometimes, just knowing you can leave if you want to helps you stick with a job until it's over. It's reassuring to know that all you have to do is call your temp coordinator and ask for a replacement. Your recruiter will talk to you and the company you're working for to see if there's any way to resolve the problem. If there isn't, you're out of there. You won't be the first person to quit an assignment, and you won't be the last. It's one of the advantages of temping. Once again, I'm not advising you to quit an assignment unless you really have to, but it helps to know you *can*. (See *Setting Limits,* later in this chapter, for more on the subject.)

DON'T BUY INTO SOMEONE ELSE'S CRISIS

Chances are, if you feel overwhelmed on an assignment it's because people around you are stressed out and are passing their anxiety on to you. Temps are usually sent to companies when the staff is overloaded. It wouldn't make much sense to call for temps when there's nothing to do.

Keep in mind that it's easy to get caught up in a company's drama when you're a new temp, especially if you're unsure of your abilities. After a few assignments, though, you'll have met enough hysterical people to realize that every workplace has stressful situations and, despite the staff's indications to the contrary, the world isn't coming to an end.

As time goes on, you will learn to relax and stop approaching each assignment as if it were a true measure of your worth. The stress will dissipate. In fact, after a while you might find that you experience far less stress as a temp than you would at a full-time job.

One valuable lesson I learned as a temp is that people lose their perspective when they're too caught up in their jobs. If there's a crisis where you're working (and there often will be), you'll inevitably deal with people who are convinced it's the worst crisis the universe has ever known. As a temp, you'll see the same hysteria over and over again, and after a while you might even find that your attitudes toward work have changed forever. Consider how many people you know who wind up with ulcers or heart attacks because of job stress.

If you stay with temporary work for a while, you'll eventually walk into yet another stressful situation, remain calm, pitch in and help out, and then walk away without a care in the world, leaving all the company's problems and stress behind you. Once you've reached this point, you'll understand why many people balk at the notion of ever working full time again.

According to Michael R. Losey, president and CEO of the Society for Human Resource Management, "Temporary workers are accustomed to rapidly changing circumstances and 'keeping their cool' under pressure, which means they can often walk into situations where they are able to make order out of chaos, thereby giving [the permanent] staff psychological as well as practical support."[16]

YOU CAN'T FAIL

It's up to your temp coordinator to match your skills with the assignment. If he or she doesn't do that, it's not your fault. You haven't failed. You're just on the wrong assignment. All you have to do on a temporary assignment is your very best. If you make an effort to help and are conscientious, hardworking, and easy to get along with, there's no way you can fail.

TEMPING TIP

If it is in no way your fault that a temp assignment didn't work out, you may be entitled to partial compensation for your time, but you may have to be assertive and ask for it.

It's best to know what your temp help company's policy is in case you are mismatched to an assignment. I've been sent on assignments only to find that the client company had changed its mind about getting a temp to do a project or that another temp help company had beaten mine in filling the order and the client had not bothered to call my company to cancel.

These are clear-cut cases warranting at least partial reimbursement, yet a temp company may balk at the idea of paying a temp when the company didn't make any money on the project. Be ready to calmly state your case. You're probably not going to be in a good mood if you get to an assignment and it's cancelled for whatever reason, but it's in your best interest to keep your cool.

NO OBLIGATION TO TAKE AN ASSIGNMENT

Remember, you don't have to take any assignment if you feel you can't handle it. Although coordinators want to place only truly qualified people in assignments, I've known some to get so caught up in beating out the competition that they'll gamble that you can do the job for the sake of filling the order. And you, too, might gamble that you can do the job in order to please your coordinator and satisfy your image of yourself as a can-do person. Watch out for this.

Accepting a challenge is one thing; it can help you stretch and build skills and confidence. But allowing yourself to get in over your head can be damaging to your self-esteem if you're then let go. Worse, you'll lose money in the resulting down time. Ask lots of questions about what will be expected of you. You know better than anyone else what your capabilities are.

MOST PEOPLE ARE UNDERSTANDING

Everyone has faced the first day on the job, and we all know how stressful new situations can be. No one expects you to perform miracles. They simply need help with a project and hope you can lend a hand.

No matter what the job, if you give 100 percent to it, you'll be appreciated. In fact, you'll be called back to work at the same company again and again, and if a job becomes available, the company will think of you first.

YOU'LL HAVE HELP

You're not going to find yourself alone with no idea of what is expected of you. Someone will show you step by step exactly what to do, and most likely there will be people all around you who are willing to answer your questions.

IT WILL GET EASIER

Once you've gained confidence in your abilities, you will relax and, believe it or not, even enjoy yourself.

YOU'LL MAKE NEW FRIENDS

You'll meet new people whom you'll become friends with, and you'll get a close-up look at how a variety of workplaces operate. Plus you'll have the satisfaction of knowing you've been helpful. In fact, the only regret of most temporary workers I've met is that they continually have to say goodbye to people they've worked with and have come to like.

Even though you'll be in a temporary situation, when you work side by side with people eight hours a day, you can't help but get to know them. You become part of the company family for a while. You know your co-workers' troubles, their jokes, their frustrations, their hopes, and their dreams, and they know yours. I've left many assignments after a round of hugs and misty eyes, and to this day I think of many of those people fondly.

On the practical side, I've also often left temporary assignments with letters of recommendation and the knowledge that if I need a job, I have lots of people I can call.

THE IMAGE ISSUE

It's no secret that temporary workers have had to fight an image problem over the years. As Jane, the nurse anesthesiologist (introduced in chapter 1) who specializes in open-heart surgery and accepts assignments through a service, remarked, "I would never call myself a temp. It sounds like I fill in when the 'real' nurse anesthesiologist is on vacation, which is hardly the case."

Jane is not alone in her dislike of the word temp. As we've said, the terminology used in association with temporary work is inadequate. It's outdated, misleading, and can have a decidedly negative connotation no matter what level you're at professionally.

As the temporary help service industry evolves and more and more people at all levels work on a temporary basis, the stigma will disappear. (Some insist it already has.) But until then, can you work as a temp and keep your self-respect intact? Yes—if you adopt the right attitude and approach.

One way to handle the negative connotations of temp work is to refer to yourself not as a temp but as a contract professional, interim worker, company doctor, interim manager, line consultant, or even business commando! But while you can use whatever term you like, doing so won't really solve the image problem; it will merely camouflage it.

The people I've met who thrive as temporary workers fight any lingering image problem or stigma associated with temporary work by putting it in the proper perspective.

DON'T FORGET WHO YOU ARE

People naturally tend to define themselves by what they do for a living. If you're not just out of school and have held a full-time job, that full-time job gave you an identity. When people you were introduced to asked, "What do you do?" you could answer with something like "I work for Gadget Company." You didn't even have to say exactly what you did at Gadget Company. You could jump right into the high points. "We manufacture more gadgets than any company in the world," you could say. "In fact, we just signed a contract . . . " You know how these conversations go.

But what do you say when you don't have a full-time job any-more?

If you were previously a teacher, for instance, and are currently doing temp work, do you say "I'm a temp"? No. Not because being a temp is anything to apologize for. It isn't. It's just that working as a temp does not define who you are. If you were a teacher, you still are a teacher. You have the degree. You know how to teach. You may very well teach again. Only now you're working on a temporary basis.

In a letter to the editor of the *Boston Globe,* a professional woman described her transition from a Washington, D.C., market-ing director with her own office and staff to a temp who answered phones. Other temps she was working with also had professional backgrounds. "In previous lives," wrote the woman, "many of us had our own offices. Now we just sit outside [someone else's] door and answer the phone."

She does make the experience seem pretty grim, and I'm sure it was—for her. But if you look at temporary work as a tool you're using, not as a definition of who you are, it doesn't have to be ego-deflating.

TEMPING TIP

If you don't like defining yourself as a temp, interim worker, or whatever, don't. Define yourself by your chosen occupation, even if you're not in it at the moment.

Temping is not an occupation, even though people may call themselves temps. Even if you become a "career temp," it's still just a working condition. It's unlikely that you'd define yourself as a full-time worker, so why call yourself a temp worker?

IT'S ALL IN YOUR ATTITUDE

I think Pat Fuller, the New York City temp (originally from Portland, Maine) I mentioned earlier, has the right attitude. She's a writer (she has a screenplay and a science fiction novel in the works) as well as a singer and songwriter. "I'm one of those New Yorkers who is really a 'something else,'" she said. "You can find them in droves here—waitresses waiting for an acting break, tele-marketers who play guitar in rock bands at night, receptionists working on screenplays. That's why I chose temping—it's the best way I know to make a career-level living without the devotion that a career demands.

"It's almost like leading a double life. Not everyone's successful at it; it requires a little grit, a sense of humor, or maybe a spirit of adventure. When you head out the door in the morning with a scribbled address in your hand, you never know what you're going to walk into."[17]

Lawyers on temporary assignments are still lawyers. Engineers on temporary assignments are still engineers. Your past achievements are not now negated just because you are not currently working in that capacity on a full-time basis.

This is not just an exercise in semantics. One of the most important things you'll have to consider when deciding if you could succeed as a temporary worker, even on a short-term basis, is your ego. Attitude makes all the difference.

SETTING LIMITS

Downsizing, right sizing, lean and mean—all those terms that mean severe cutbacks in full-time jobs have taken their toll on the collective American workers' psyche. Few people today feel totally secure about their job, and as a consequence they're compromising far more than they used to. If you still have a full-time job, are you so grateful that you put up with a lot more abuse than you want to?

When you are a temporary worker, if a boss or co-worker is unfair or even abusive, it becomes vibrantly clear to you—maybe for the first time in your working life—that you don't have to try to adjust to the situation.

You *don't* have to swallow your pride and keep your mouth shut; you *don't* have to lose sleep and let off steam by endlessly discussing your mistreatment with your colleagues, your family, the human resources department, and your friends. You *don't* have to carefully consider the impact quitting your job will have on your family, career, and future. If you don't like the way you're being treated, you just walk. Think of how liberating it can feel just knowing you have that option!

The one time I ran into a truly ego-crushing, verbally abusive boss on a temporary assignment, I had the great satisfaction of saying "No." Not only that, her staff also had the great satisfaction of hearing me say no—something they would have loved to do for themselves if only they dared risk their jobs. From the looks on their faces and the secret thumbs-up gestures, I got the feeling that the entire staff wanted to pop open a bottle of champagne and carry me out on their shoulders.

I have to admit that even though I was furious, I did call my temporary help coordinator first to let her know what was happening. I knew if I simply walked off the job I would not work for that temp company again, and I saw no reason why I should suffer because of this woman's bad behavior.

As it turned out, I was the second person the temp company had sent to this woman—and the last. The company refused to send a replacement for me. Yes, it was a question of principles, but it also made good business sense. Temp help companies compete for the best temporary personnel. They want a pool of "career temps" they can count on. Obviously, subjecting personnel to abuse is neither a good retention tool nor a morale booster, and it's not worth the trouble.

"There are just some things that a person who has self-respect will not do. Period. End. No matter what the risk or payoff," Nancy O'Brien, a temp help coordinator at Pinch Hitters, Inc. in Pittsburgh, tells her temporary employees. "It's good to have that in mind before you start to work," she says, "but even in the event of a real disaster, don't just leave an assignment, even with just cause. If you feel that you simply cannot stay there, at the very least call us first and ask us to replace you as soon as possible. It is just plain embarrassing to have the client call and inquire about your whereabouts."[18]

WHEN TO REFUSE AN ASSIGNMENT

Chances are you're going to be offered assignments you'll love and assignments you're not going to like at all. The beauty of temporary work is that you don't have to take any job you don't want. You can politely decline. But how often can you decline assignments before your coordinator stops calling you and starts calling someone else who is less fussy?

In the beginning, when you're establishing a relationship and a reputation with temporary help companies, your main goal is to prove:

- you're an ace at what you do
- you're easy and pleasant to work with
- you won't to be too fussy about jobs
- you're not going to panic

- you're someone coordinators can rely on to do a good job
- you'll say yes when called at the last minute
- you're a professional who will make the temp company look good
- you're a survivor, even in difficult circumstances
- you're someone clients like
- you give 100 percent
- you're relaxed enough to reassure clients

ALTERNATIVES TO TEMPING WITH A TEMP HELP COMPANY

If you're not sure temping as I've described it is for you, you might want to consider one of the following alternatives.

IN-HOUSE POOLS

If you don't think you could handle the stress of constantly walking into a new work situation (and many people can't) but would still like the flexibility of temporary work, you might consider working as a temp in a company or hospital's in-house pool—assuming you have top-notch skills to offer.

In-house pools are now popular in many large companies, much to the dismay of some temp help companies. Temporary staffing has always been used in the biggest companies and hospitals, but lately, instead of calling a temp help or locum tenens company when departments request additional assistance, the bigger companies and hospitals simply draw from their own pool of per diem or temporary help. Some of these in-house "temps" are former full-time workers who want to stay with the company but would like relief from the nine-to-five grind. Others are recruited from the outside.

The advantages to companies are obvious. By relying on trained temps who are familiar with the job and organization, firms and hospitals can keep their full-time staff to a minimum and pay only for the hours temp employees work, all the while maintaining continuity and eliminating the need for constant training.

Some companies and hospitals set up their own temporary coordinators; others sign an agreement with a temp help company to handle all the operational details of scheduling temps from within the facility.

IN-HOUSE POOLS: PROS AND CONS

Pros

- Benefits may be provided.
- You'll have scheduling flexibility without a constant change in work site.
- There's more job continuity than with regular temping.
- You'll experience less of the stress that comes with a constant change in environment.
- There may be opportunities for cross-training.
- It's an easy way to enter or exit a big company.
- You may be eligible for company-paid continuing education.
- You'll have more chances for getting to know fellow workers and making friends than with regular temping.

Cons

- Work environments and jobs are less varied.
- You'll have fewer chances to learn new skills.
- It's not as easy to spot opportunities and make job contacts.
- Boredom may be a problem because projects are routine or offer few challenges.
- There's more risk of getting involved in office politics than with regular temping.
- Competition for the best assignments may be heated.

The advantages to you, the temp, are many. When you work for one company's pool, you have the best of both worlds—flexibility plus stability. If you're trying to juggle school, work, and a family, a flexible schedule without the stress of constantly changing work environments or constantly hustling and negotiating for assignments could be just what you're looking for.

You could also make more money than with a temp help company and maintain a steady hourly or daily rate, since the company or hospital isn't paying the temp help company's fee in addition to yours—but this isn't necessarily so. Health benefits may also be provided if you work a certain number of hours (usually at least 30 each week), and you may have access to any continuing education or in-service seminars available to regular employees.

Besides making lasting friends (one of the best parts of any job), another advantage is the cross-training you're likely to get—valuable no matter what you plan to do in the future. In-house pools are good ways for people to enter and exit a big company. If you're at retirement age but want to keep on working for the company on a more flexible basis, a pool might work for you. Or if you're looking for full-time employment and you're brought on to work in the pool, you'll be first on the list of people to be considered when the company or hospital is hiring.

Signing up with an in-house pool may be as simple as sending in a resume (you'll be interviewed prior to an assignment) or may involve an initial interview, a battery of tests, and a medical exam.

Now the down side. Although most hospitals and companies will try to keep you as busy as you want to be, you aren't guaranteed an assignment. As in-house pools become more popular with people looking for temp work, the best assignments go quickly. One occupational therapist I know who works in a hospital pool said many per diem workers line up as soon as the week's per diem jobs are posted so they can get the best hours. What's left are often graveyard shifts no one else wants.

Lisa Noe, a traveling nurse from Hamden, Connecticut, said she rarely gets turned down by her hospital pool when she wants to work between travel assignments, but she's heard from other nurses that steady work from in-house pools is getting harder to come by.

If you've just signed up with an in-house pool, the company is, understandably, going to be more loyal to those who've worked in the pool for a while, even if you're more skilled. I never got a call from a hospital pool I signed up with, although the same hospital called me to interview for a full-time job.

In some ways, believe it or not, working in an in-house pool can be more stressful than working for a temp service. Since you stay at the same company or hospital, you could end up getting involved with at least some of the office politics. (Try to imagine hearing this from a fellow temp: "How come you got that assignment when I've been here longer?")

FLOATING

Although it's not really temporary work, I include floating here because it's sometimes confused with working as a temp in an in-house pool. The big difference between the two is that floaters are company employees and temps are not.

As a floater, you have a lot more security than you do in an in-house pool. You work for a company, perhaps on a flexible or part-time basis, performing different jobs and filling in as needed. Unlike a temp in a pool, you'll still be paid by the company even if there's nothing to do (a rarity).

Big law firms often have secretaries who move around from office to office, going where the work is; newspapers have reporters who float; and colleges often have versatile staff members who can take on different projects for different departments as needed.

Depending on how often and how far you're moved, floating can be as stressful as or even more stressful than temping, at least in the beginning. When you're a temp, you'll go to the same office every day until the assignment is over. But as a floater, you may be moved from office to office, building to building, or site to site daily.

Just when you get used to one job and one group of people, you're sent somewhere else to do a different job with a different group of people. You might not even have a desk and won't know from week to week what your phone extension is or sometimes even what town you'll be in.

Twice, for a year at a time, I floated as a newspaper reporter; the work was hard but definitely interesting. Rather than cover a "beat," where I'd look for news in a town I was familiar with, I was on the road looking for "breaking news" in unfamiliar towns every day. I spent a great deal of time and energy finding my way around and scrambling to learn who was who before I could even begin to work. Still, I was never bored, and I felt less constricted than when I was supervised by one boss.

FLOATING: PROS AND CONS

Pros

- You'll have both job security and constant change and challenge.
- Benefits are usually provided.
- You'll usually be exposed to less office politics than regular employees are.
- There will often be opportunities for cross-training.
- You'll have more independence and less supervision than regular employees do.

Cons

- Regularly changing departments and sometimes buildings or sites can be stressful.
- It's hard to stay organized without a permanent base of operation.
- You'll have less control over the type of work you do than regular employees have.
- Often you won't really feel a part of a group of workers.
- You may miss the satisfaction of seeing a project completed.
- There's pressure to learn quickly.
- You'll constantly have to adjust to different management styles.

INDEPENDENT CONTRACTING OR FREELANCING

If you're successful as a temp, sooner or later you'll probably realize that you could make more money working for yourself than by getting assignments through a temporary help company. So many people are working on their own these days that independent contractors are now temp help companies' biggest competition. It's great to be your own boss and keep all the money a client company pays for your services, but consider the advantages and the drawbacks carefully before you strike out on your own.

Freelancing Versus Temping

Before you become an independent contractor, compare freelancing with temping:

- Temporary work eliminates the need for an accountant who's up to date in tax laws. Accountants cost money. Will you still make a profit as a freelancer? Or, if you do the paperwork yourself, how much of your time will it take? Time is money.
- As a temporary worker you usually get a paycheck every week. As a freelancer you may have to chase a client to get paid.
- It takes time to market your skills and set up assignments. Are you going to experience downtime or are you going to arrange new assignments while you're working? Since you're only one person, how are you going to keep your clients happy if you can't help them when they need you because you're busy with an assignment for someone else?
- Who's going to act as bill collector when clients don't pay on time or don't pay at all? Can you afford to wait for payment? When are you going to make collection calls?
- What about workers' compensation and unemployment insurance? As an independent contractor, you aren't eligible for some benefits temps and full-time workers have. Clients may worry about what will happen if you're injured on the job. Will you have no recourse but to sue?

This is not to say you shouldn't freelance. For some people it turns out to be an excellent choice. Many have made valuable contacts through temping assignments that they can use to start their own freelance businesses. But you must weigh the advantages against the headaches of being your own boss.

INDEPENDENT CONTRACTING OR FREELANCING: PROS AND CONS

Pros

- You can often make better money than when working for a temp help company.
- You may have more job satisfaction as your own boss.
- You have control over which projects you take.
- There's no one to answer to but yourself.
- You're free to work when and where you want.
- You'll have opportunities to build your business.

Cons

- There are no paid benefits.
- You must keep all your own records.
- You'll have to hustle for work.
- You may not get paid regularly.

EMPLOYEE LEASING

Some small businesses turn to an arrangement called employee leasing, usually when they find they can't afford to pay their employees benefits. In a leasing arrangement, a company's employees may be "fired" and then hired by a leasing company, which leases the employees back to the original employer. The employer no longer has to provide benefits such as liability taxes, workers' compensation, or disability and unemployment insurance because it now leases, rather than employs, its workers. Employee benefits are paid by the leasing company.

Employee leasing is not an option you choose but rather a strategy your employer might use. You may, however, have opportunities to be recruited by an employee leasing company to work for a client company. Since a leasing company's strength is its ability to buy good insurance at a reduced rate because of the volume of employees involved, the leasing companies are able to attract the best employees.

CHAPTER 4

Getting Started

Most people get started as temporary workers in exactly the same way—the wrong way. It's only after they're experienced and have made costly mistakes that they finally understand there is more to temporary work than they thought.

You don't have to make the same mistakes most people make if you keep a few points in mind before you get started. Quite simply, you must plan your strategy by doing your research and be prepared when signing up with temp help companies.

PLAN YOUR STRATEGY

Most people stumble onto temporary work. I did myself. I was between jobs, having moved from Houston to the Boston area, and I needed work in a hurry. My background was in the editorial end of publishing, which, at the time, was not flourishing. When I saw a temporary help company ad for office workers, I called on impulse, rushed over, and found myself seated in a temp help coordinator's office, politely waiting to be offered clerical work.

I had only a vague idea of what clerical workers did. I didn't have a clue about what I was looking for in temp work, what kind of assignments were available, what the going rates were, what skills were necessary, or anything else. What's worse, when the coordinator asked me what my office skills were, I was at a loss. In fact, I wasn't sure I *had* any office skills. I'd always had editorial jobs, aside from my early years as a waitress.

As far as I knew, I could write and carry trays—and that was about it. I didn't see any point in taking a typing test since I didn't have a secretarial background and had no practical training except for a typing course in high school.

Fortunately, it was a good market for temps at the time, and although I was giving absolutely no help to my coordinator, she was undaunted. After a series of tests and pertinent questions, she decided that I actually did have marketable skills for temp work. As this first coordinator pointed out, my previous jobs had given me useful experience working with people and on the phone. And I had used a computer before (although it wasn't a type commonly used in business), which meant I knew the basics and could type. (As it turned out, the typing test showed I had unknowingly built up a very fast speed, which opened a lot of doors for me.)

Back in the late 70s there weren't as many options in professional fields as there are now, so I looked no further and was delighted to know that I was qualified for temporary work and would be called when an assignment came in. I don't even think I mentioned money when I interviewed at my first temp help company, or, if I did, I was probably told payment depended on what the job entailed, and I let it go at that. Then I went home and waited for my phone to ring.

If you don't realize it already, you'll see after reading this chapter that each step I took was the wrong step. Lots of people continue to make these same mistakes and then tell me they've tried temping but nothing ever came of it. Well, of course not. If I used this same strategy—or, really, lack of strategy—now, I'd still be waiting for a coordinator to call me. Let's look at a better way.

DO YOUR RESEARCH

If you're an experienced job shopper, you know that finding the right job takes research and preparation. You have your resume up

SAMPLE LIST OF TEMPORARY POSITIONS
ADVERTISED NATIONWIDE

Accountants
Art gallery professionals
Assemblers
Attorneys
Auto mechanics
Baby-sitters
Bilingual personnel
Bookkeepers
Butlers
Cafeteria help
Cashiers
Chauffeurs
Chefs
Chemists
Clerical workers
Computer graphics artists
Construction help
Customer service reps
Data processing operators
Demonstrators
Dental technicians
Dentists
Desktop publishing artists
Engineers
Factory workers
Food and beverage workers
Gal and guy Fridays
Hospital administrators
Hospital researchers
Hotel/travel management and trainees
Housekeepers
Human resources specialists
Hygienists
Inventory help
Kitchen help
Laboratory technicians
Laborers

Landscapers
Machinists
Maids
Mail room help
Marketing professionals
Mechanics
Movers
Musicians
Nurses
Office managers
Opticians
Packers
Paralegals
Physicians
Porters
Production workers
Programmers
Proofreaders
Public relations specialists
Real estate professionals
Receptionists
Record managers
Sales executives
Sales managers
Sales trainees
Secretaries
Stock people
Switchboard operators
Ticketers
Tool and die makers
Truck helpers
Typesetters
Wait staff
Warehouse workers
Word processor operators
X-ray technicians

to date, you know as much as you can about the company you're applying to, you've decided on your bottom salary figure, and you've assessed the skills that make you a good candidate for the job. When you walk into a job interview, you are dressed professionally, have all your questions ready, have anticipated questions you'll be asked, and are prepared to negotiate.

Applying for temporary work should be no different than applying for a full-time job. You take the same sorts of steps. Here's how:

CHOOSE THE RIGHT TEMP HELP COMPANIES FOR YOU

The kind of temporary help companies you should sign up with will depend on the skills you have to offer as a temporary worker. If you're an engineer you'll obviously want to sign up with temp help companies that specialize in that field; if you're a nurse you'll want to look for a service that places nurses; and so on. (I'll be discussing temporary opportunities with the more specialized, industry-specific temp help companies in later chapters, especially in chapter 8.) If your skills aren't so specialized, you'll want to sign up with a "traditional" temp company that places a full range of general-skilled temporary help. I've compiled a sampling of positions that temp help companies across the nation have advertised to give you an idea of what's available; see the box (on page 61).

Even if you are a professional with high-level skills, you may want to sign up with both "traditional" temporary help companies and specialized companies. In addition to your advanced skills, consider using what Heather Patay, executive vice president of Talent Resources Company, Inc. in Northbrook, Illinois, calls your "subskills." Patay recently placed one woman whose story illustrates why signing up with both types of companies can be a good idea.

Patay explained, "Kathy was an English major who had been looking for temporary work in the usual editorial fields—advertising, publishing, public relations, and so on—and wasn't having much luck." Much to Kathy's surprise, a temporary proofreading assignment Patay arranged for her resulted in a job offer Kathy was happy to accept: an interesting, decent-paying position as a corporate historian and librarian for a food manufacturing firm. Although managing a fairly extensive corporate library and researching and writing information for executives is a job that often goes to English majors, "it wasn't something Kathy would have considered or even known about," said Patay.

As a professional you might also find that travel or even relocation is required for many assignments with specialized temp help companies. If neither possibility appeals to you, you might be better off concentrating on the many full-service temp help companies that place temps of all skills and levels.

DETERMINE WHERE THE JOBS ARE

Find out how many temporary help companies are in your area so you'll know if there's going to be enough work to keep you in assignments. Obviously, the more temporary help companies there are, the more work there is. If there are very few, if any, such companies in your area, though, it probably means there are also few full-time jobs, so you may have to think about broadening your horizons.

TEMPING TIP

It'll save you a lot of work and time later if you use a loose-leaf notebook—preferably one that you can carry with you once you're working—to store the information you gather. (I'll talk more about how to use a notebook later in this chapter and also in chapter 5.)

CITIES OR SUBURBS?

If you live in a big city, you should have plenty of temporary help companies to choose from. Your biggest problem will be deciding which ones to sign up with. If you live in the suburbs, though, you won't have as many options. If the companies you do have in your area include divisions of a national chain, that's a good sign.

Presumably, a lot of market research goes on before a national company sets up shop, so if you see branches of big companies advertising for temporary help, there is work nearby.

If you find, though, as I did, that your suburban temporary help companies are small and few in number, you may have to augment your local assignments with temporary work in the cities closest to you. Whether you will or not depends on how good you are at what you do, whether there's work in your field, and whether you take on a long-term assignment. I know most people hate the very idea of commuting, but before you dismiss it altogether, consider the pluses. There are several.

For one thing, wages are usually higher in the city, and there is a much greater variety of assignments to choose from. I found there were also a lot more assignments available in the city on a daily, rather than weekly, basis, which helps if you need time to attend to other important matters during the week, such as interviews for full-time jobs, children's appointments, or classes. If you're an actor and need to audition for a part on Wednesday, for instance, and have a dress rehearsal on Thursday, you might pick up work for Monday, Tuesday, and Friday. It's tricky to arrange, but it can be done.

So when you think about commuting, remember that you may not have to travel five days a week. Especially if you have clerical skills, you could land a three-day assignment locally and a two-day assignment in the city, either on a one-time or a long-term basis. I've done it.

Of course, you have to consider the cost of commuting and the time you spend on the road, but you could still come out ahead. I used to make $8 to $10 an hour in the country and $10 to $14 in the city as a word processing secretary. This was before the recession and after I'd learned over a dozen software languages and won over a few new clients for temporary help companies.

Extra-short assignments from the city were always good to fall back on when the only work I was offered in the country paid less than my bottom hourly rate. I felt it was important to be firm and stick to my bottom figure no matter what, so rather than take less money, I'd work in the city, sending the message to my regular temp help company that I did have other options and wasn't so desperate for work that I'd take any assignment for any salary.

TEMPING TIP

Even if you live in the suburbs or out in the country and don't want to commute to work, it's a good idea to be registered with at least one temp help company in the nearest city as an emergency backup for when local assignments are not as plentiful as you'd like and you really need more income.

Is there a prestigious company in the city you'd love to work for, but you want to keep your commute to a minimum? Consider commuting for a short-term assignment with such a firm between local assignments. If you're entering or reentering the job market and have office skills, the experience of working for a prestigious big-city corporation can help build your resume—and your confidence—quickly.

If you live in the city and want a change of environment, you can also investigate commuting into the suburbs or the country for work. Some of the bigger temporary help assignments are far-reaching or have branches in suburbia.

PINPOINTING TEMP HELP COMPANIES

Basically, there are three places to look for the names of temporary help companies:

- help wanted ads
- the yellow pages of your phone book
- trade magazines

Start with the help wanted section of your local newspapers and the yellow pages. If you live in the country or suburbs and think you're going to have to commute at least occasionally, visit your library and get out all the phone books and newspapers for your area. If you have specialized skills, get out copies of the trade magazines for your field to see if temporary help companies advertise in them.

In the phone books, look under "employment" and make two copies of all the temporary help company listings. You'll want to keep one copy of the ads in the yellow pages intact and in alphabetical order in your temping notebook for easy reference later (see the temping tip earlier in this chapter and also chapter 5 for more about keeping a notebook). The other you will cut up. You should also make one copy of the newspaper advertisements for temporary help—and for full-time work, even if you're not looking for a full-time position.

Now clip every ad listing work in your field from one of your yellow pages copies and from your newspaper and trade magazine ads. Tape them, arranged in groups by type of work offered, in your notebook, leaving plenty of room for notes. You could have one page of companies specializing in your top-level skills, for instance, and another page for companies that specialize in your "subskills," if you have both.

Keep in mind that temporary help companies don't always advertise in the newspapers every week, so you'll have to keep watching your newspapers for new ads. But for now, you have enough material to start your research.

When you see all the ads together, a pattern should emerge, giving you an idea of the work that's out there and the skills that are in demand in your region for people in your line of work.

When you look over the newspaper listings, you may see great pay rates and jobs listed. Don't get too excited about these jobs and wages until you investigate further. Some companies use hooks to attract your interest. When you inquire, you may find that the top rates are reserved for people who have been with the company for some time and that the fabulous assignment you read about has been filled. This is not always the case—sometimes the jobs are for real—but it's something to keep in mind.

Highlight assignments that interest you, even if you think you're underqualified for the job. When you call a temporary help company, this information can help you be more specific about the kind of work you're looking for and give the coordinator a better idea of your skills. Highlighting specific jobs and qualifications should also help you inventory your skills, give you ideas about temporary work you can do, and help you decide which companies to call first.

Don't be intimidated by the jobs and skills listed in the ads. What you see will be the jobs and skills most in demand. Most temporary help companies also have a full range of other assignments requiring various levels of skills, and chances are you'll be qualified for many of them.

Now you're ready to start making appointments.

SIGNING UP

"It's best to sign up with a few agencies that have good reputations," advises Heather Patay of Talent Resources. "Not many agencies have enough work for everyone all the time, plus you run the risk of being pigeonholed by one company. You might get a reputation for being good at CAD/CAM assignments, for instance, and get no other type of work from that company, when what you're really looking for is work as a design engineer. A diversity of agencies may provide a diversity of assignments."

Pat Brie, owner of J. R. Personnel/AID Temporary, a temp help company in Peabody, Massachusetts, agrees. "I always tell people to sign up with many companies in the beginning. I know a lot of other companies don't tell people this because they're competitive, but we're a small company. I can't keep everyone working all the time. I don't want to be responsible for people's working lives. Besides, eventually they'll establish relationships with coordinators and be able to rely on a few good temporary help companies to keep them in work. They shouldn't worry about how that will happen. It will just evolve," she says.

Once you're happy with a temporary help company and it's

happy with you, it's best to stick with that firm so you can take advantage of any benefits you'll be entitled to after you've worked for it for a certain length of time. But in the beginning it's a good idea to sign up with as many temporary help companies as you can.

Even when I was established as a temp and was turning down work, I continued to register with companies whenever it was convenient. If I found myself working nearby an untried temp company, for example, I'd register there during my lunch hour. Sometimes the process took two lunch hours—one for the interview, the second for the testing—but it was worth it. (I'll discuss signing up later in this chapter.)

The more companies you're registered with, the more assignments you'll be offered. Each company has regular clients who use its services exclusively. In fact, if you want to work at a particular company, there's nothing wrong with asking the human resources department which temporary help company it uses so you can sign up with that one.

If a temporary help company is desperate to find someone with a particular skill a client wants and you have that skill, registering with many agencies will give you bargaining power to keep your rate high. You'll learn how to negotiate later, but for now, start making those appointments!

SHOULD YOU REVEAL THAT YOU'VE SIGNED UP WITH OTHER TEMP HELP COMPANIES?

You probably don't want to spook temporary help companies by making it known that you're signing up with a lot of companies, just as you wouldn't tell potential full-time employers that you are applying for many other jobs.

The competition can be fierce in the temporary service industry, and coordinators prefer temps who are going to represent their company exclusively, especially if they're highly skilled. You can imagine how embarrassing it would be for a temp help company to brag to a top client about you only to find you worked for that same client last week through another temp company. Rather than take that risk, your temp coordinator may call someone who's not as good but has been working for the company pretty much exclusively.

So what do you do when the application asks for a list of other temp help companies you've signed with? Lie, as one temp suggested to me?

Well, you probably won't go to jail if you don't list every temp help company you signed up with (although the application is considered a legal document), but I prefer to be honest and direct with the people I'm dealing with. For one thing, you're bound to be discovered eventually; and for another, you lose bargaining power you may need later.

Here's what I do:

Before I fill out an application form, I ask the coordinator if I can speak frankly—and I do. I say that I don't want to lie but feel uncomfortable listing other companies I've signed up with in the past because I'm afraid it will prevent me from getting work if the company is competitive.

I explain that I'm looking for one good company to build a relationship with, and I reassure the coordinator that I don't want to jeopardize the relationship by embarrassing the company. Then I ask for advice on how I can avoid doing that.

Finally, I spell out what I'm looking for as far as rates and assignments go and add that if I get what I want, I will be glad to work exclusively for the company.

Of course, I try to be as friendly and tactful as possible. I've always found that temp help companies respond to my openness by being open in return. This eliminates any second-guessing about what temp help companies expect, and it makes for a workable business relationship.

PLANNING FOR INTERVIEWS

How much time you spend interviewing at each temp help company is going to depend on your field. Some companies require extensive testing, which can take a lot of time. For clerical or light industrial assignments, I'd count on at least one or two hours at each company.

When calling to set up an interview, ask how long the interview and testing process will take so that you can plan your time accordingly.

Signing up at two companies a day is probably all you're going to be able to handle, although if the companies are close together you may be able to squeeze in three interviews. But it's best not to overbook yourself and have to reschedule an appointment after you've made it—that's starting out on the wrong foot.

MAKING APPOINTMENTS

Don't expect to learn much from a temporary help company over the phone unless the company "sells" out-of-state specialized skills. No matter what you ask, the response will usually be "That depends." Usually you've got to apply in person. When you call for an appointment, be prepared to highlight your skills quickly. Have your notebook handy for reference. Your resume too.

Be positive. Don't immediately go into the reasons why you're no longer working for a particular company, if that's the case. Simply state that you're interested in temporary work and spell out your skills. Write them down ahead of time so you don't forget anything. Use the present tense. Don't say something like "I was an accountant before I got laid off." Instead, say "I'm an accountant with ten years' experience. I specialize in finance, but I'm also experienced in information systems, payroll, accounts receivable, and accounts payable—you name it, I've done it." If you saw an ad for an assignment you think you're qualified for, mention it.

BE PREPARED WHEN YOU CALL

It may sound like I'm making a simple process complicated, but you should be prepared to ask—and answer—appropriate questions when calling temporary help companies to request an interview. The fact is, at many temporary help companies that first phone call is an initial screening.

While you're outlining your skills, the company representative is forming a first impression of you:

- Are you articulate enough to impress potential clients?
- Do you have appropriate skills?
- Do you sound self-assured and confident of your abilities?
- Are you prepared when you make the call?
- Do you know what you want to get across?

If you can't quickly outline what you can do for a temporary help company, you might not even get in for an interview. Coordinators don't want to waste your time or theirs.

TEMPING TIP

When you make that initial call, keep in mind that telephone skills are an important part of many temporary assignments. How you sound over the phone does *count.*

Pat Brie from J. R. Personnel/AID Temporary, introduced earlier in this chapter, says, "I can tell within the first minute if someone's going to work out or not. Successful applicants know what they want to say. They're prepared."

Consider the traits that impress you when you call a company. What makes someone sound professional? You don't have to be a great orator, but being prepared and having information about your subject—you—in front of you will certainly help. That way you're not going to be caught making thinking noises like "ummm" or "ahh" while searching your memory for the names of the computer languages you know or the positions you've held.

TEMPING TIP

If the temp help company also has a full-time employment place-ment division, by all means sign up with both divisions, even if you're only looking for temporary work at the moment.

It'll be well worth your time and effort to sign up with both the temporary help division and the full-time division. People from temporary help companies I haven't thought of in years still call me when a job requiring my particular skills comes across their desks. (You'll be amazed how long your application stays in some of these files.) Some job searchers have even called me at my full-time position to tempt me with a job, especially when they knew it paid more than what I was making. (How did they know what I was making? I told them when I took the job. As a courtesy I deac-tivated my file so that no one wasted time considering me for jobs I couldn't take.)

Even if you don't pursue any of the leads you are given, it's valuable to know what jobs are "out there" and what salaries other people in your field are commanding. It's also comforting to know you have options.

TEMPING TIP

Don't confuse these free job placement services with agencies that charge a fee to find you a job. If the placement service is free, the ad will say "client paid" or words to that effect. I have nothing against employment agencies that charge a fee to find you work— but that's not what this book is concerned with.

THE INTERVIEW

When a company hires a full-time worker, there's usually a proba-tion period—ranging from three to six months—before it has to make a total commitment to that employee. The temporary worker, though, needs to be a proven quantity the first day on the assignment. This is why you can be sure your interviews for temporary work will be thorough.

Here's what to expect:

YOU WILL BE ASKED FOR REFERENCES

It's an excellent idea to contact the people you're going to list as references ahead of time. Your temp coordinator will ask permission to call these people. It's far better if you can answer "Of course" with no hesitation and total confidence than if you say something like "Ah, well, I'd better call them first to see if it's okay." If you were the coordinator, wouldn't you wonder how current these references were?

While you're speaking to your references—the people who are going to vouch for you—write down the correct spelling of their names, their full titles, and their work phone numbers (with extensions). Make sure you bring this information with you to the interview. Otherwise, you'll have to go home and call it in, which wastes time for both you and the coordinator and could give a negative first impression.

YOU WILL FILL OUT AN APPLICATION

If you're signing up with more than one temporary help company, filling out these applications can be tedious. After a while you might be tempted to take shortcuts or get sloppy. Don't do it.

Coordinators will be looking for clues about you. You're raising red flags if you're messy and your handwriting is illegible. If you leave blanks, people will wonder if you have trouble reading or following directions or, worse, have something to hide. On the other hand, don't take an inordinate amount of time to fill out the application—being too obsessive will make people wonder about how fast you work.

TEMPING TIP

Temporary help companies consider an applicant's Work History Card a legal document. You must, therefore, fill it out completely.

Make sure you bring several copies of your resume with you, preferably in an attractive folder that says you care about the impression you're making. You can ask if your resume will suffice for the work history information section. If the answer is no, submit your resume with the completed application anyway. It may contain additional information you can't fit on the application, and it will provide information at a glance when clients call and coordinators are flipping through your file.

TEMPING TIP

Condense your current, hot skills and length of experience in an overview at the top of your resume so temp help companies can easily see your qualifications at a glance, Janet Christopher of Advance Personnel Associates Inc. advises. Companies can respond more quickly if they don't have to pick through the resume looking for skills. Also, keep resumes to a maximum of two pages. It's unrealistic to expect people to spend the time required to read through a longer one.

If coordinators don't want your resume, they can always throw it away, but, once again, it shows you're serious about working and have come prepared.

YOU WILL BE TESTED

When attempting to place temporary workers at client companies, temp help companies often mention that their testing of temps is extensive. By testing thoroughly, temp companies ensure their clients that the right temp will be sent to the job.

The type of test you'll be given depends on the nature of the work you do. Obviously, engineers aren't going to be given word processing tests, and word processors aren't going to be given engineering tests. Testing varies greatly from company to company.

Some of the small companies might hand you two sheets of paper, one a math quiz and the other a grammar and spelling quiz, which you can finish in less than 20 minutes. Others have turned testing into a very sophisticated science. Depending on the kind of work you'd like to do, you may be given a battery of tests that could take from two to four hours to complete and measure everything from hand-eye coordination to your desire to do quality work.

There's not much you can do to prepare for any of these tests; your best bet is to be rested and relaxed when you take them. Either you'll score well or you won't. Keep in mind that the test is designed to determine not only what kind of work you perform well but the type of work you like most. By taking these tests you will decrease the chances of being placed in assignments you won't like or don't yet have the skills for.

TEMPING TIP

If you fail your test, you can (and should) ask to take it over. One of the best registered nurses at a major teaching hospital in Massachusetts told me she flunked her nursing test for per diem workers because it had been years since she'd had to use the formulas asked for. Once she knew what the company was looking for, she got out her old textbooks, brushed up, went back, and took the test again. The second time she got a perfect score.

It's not at all unusual to get a low score on your first test for temp work, no matter how good you are at your job. These tests are harder than most people expect. If you don't do well the first time, don't be embarrassed to try again.

YOU WILL BE INTERVIEWED

After the coordinator reviews your application, you'll sit down for an interview. If there are gaps in your employment history, be prepared to discuss them. Don't apologize for them; simply explain them.

The kinds of questions you might be asked follow. When you consider how you'd answer them, keep in mind that some of them are tricky. Be honest, but remember that your task is to appear upbeat, easy to get along with, accommodating, and dependable.

- What kind of work do you enjoy doing?
- When can you start?
- What hours can you work?
- What was your favorite job?
- What was your least favorite job and why? (Be prepared for this one.)
- What are your career goals?
- How far can you travel?
- What type of personalities do you prefer not to work with?
- How do you handle difficult people?
- How well do you perform under pressure?
- How long do you expect to be a temp?
- Are you looking for full-time work?
- If so, are you going to need time off for interviews?
- Would you consider temp-to-permanent? (This means you'll begin working for a company as a temp and then will become a permanent employee if the company likes your work. I will discuss such arrangements later in this chapter and again in chapter 6.)
- Should we call you with jobs that pay below your rate?
- Do you prefer to work alone or with people?
- Do you prefer a large company or a small company?
- Are there companies you'd like to work for? Don't want to work for?
- What fields do you like? Dislike?
- Do you prefer structured or informal companies?

- How flexible can you be in taking assignments?
- Do you prefer long- or short-term assignments?
- How well do you do taking direction?

WHAT TO CONSIDER BEFORE THE INTERVIEW

Most of the questions will be easy for you to answer. There are some common questions, though, that you might want to give some thought to ahead of time. Here are a few examples:

DO YOU WANT SHORT-TERM OR LONG-TERM ASSIGNMENTS?

You can say that it depends on the job and the salary. Then talk about what kind of job and rate you'd accept for a long-term assignment. Some temporary help companies, especially those that specialize in high-skill fields such as medicine, science, or executive placement, often place people for months or even a year at a time. Companies that handle the more traditional types of temp work, though, such as clerical and light industrial help, have assignments of all lengths—as short as half a day or as long as a year or more. So how do you know which you want?

THE PLUSES OF LONG-TERM ASSIGNMENTS

Long-term assignments usually pay more than short-term because you're making a commitment to the client company. I've always been offered better rates for long-term assignments without having to ask, but that could be because my coordinators knew me and probably figured I'd ask if they didn't offer.

If you're experienced and have a good reputation and aren't being offered a decent wage for a long-term assignment, take some time to think about the pros and cons. If you're tied up on a long-term assignment you could be passing up better pay on other assignments, a chance to explore options, a variety of job experiences, business contacts, and other opportunities.

Many experienced temporary workers (like me) prefer short-term assignments because they've become addicted to change and new challenges and get bored on long-term assignments. Short-term work is more fun!

On the plus side, long-term assignments are safer because you don't have to constantly hustle after assignments, negotiate your wages, or go through the stress of constant change. In tough economic times, when there is not enough work to go around, it's better to have long-term assignments than risk having no assignments at all. There's also the possibility that the client company will come to rely on you once you've been there for a while and will want to hire you full time (very common).

If you do a good job on a long-term assignment and the company often uses temps, you will keep getting called back as new projects and time crunches come up. The company will request you because the staff knows you're good and likes you and you already know a lot about the company. (The actual job you do may change each time you go there.) Your popularity becomes a bargaining chip, and rightly so.

If the client company *really* wants you, your coordinator will do his or her best to try to get you on that assignment, sometimes (not always) even raising your rates for fear the client will go to another temporary help company. (This might be the time to ask for a better rate if your coordinator doesn't offer it first.) If you can develop a good reputation with a few desirable companies that often use temporary workers, it's as if you're in the client company's own temporary pool and you can be more secure than lots of people with full-time jobs.

On a less practical level, you might be happier going back to companies where you've made friends. It sure makes a job more pleasant when you walk into a company and everyone's grinning because they're happy to see you and you're happy to see them. A long-term assignment can feel just like being part of the company family, except you're exempt from the politics and unpleasantries that come up when people work together year after year.

THE PLUSES OF SHORT-TERM ASSIGNMENTS

Short-term assignments also have advantages. You obviously have more job flexibility, which is crucial if you need lots of time off. If you're actively seeking a full-time job and hope to go on frequent interviews, short-term temporary assignments are usually preferable. Although most people are understanding when you are between jobs and looking for work, constantly taking off for job interviews on long-term assignments is usually frowned on.

Client companies generally ask for long-term temporaries because they'd like to avoid a lot of disruption and don't want to have to keep replacing people who leave for full-time jobs. Of course, it's always best to find out the individual company's policy regarding time off. Some companies won't care if you juggle your schedule as long as the work gets done well.

HOW FAR ARE YOU WILLING TO COMMUTE?

Think this over and have your answer ready. Be realistic. If you say 30 miles yet decline each time you're asked to take an assignment 30 miles away, you'll stop getting calls.

ARE YOU INTERESTED IN TEMP-TO-PERMANENT?

As I mentioned earlier, temp-to-permanent, as it's called, means you'll begin working for a client as a temp, and, if all goes well, after a month or so you'll be offered a full-time job. Again, the smart answer to whether or not you'd be interested is "It depends on the job." If you're looking for a permanent position, this is the best way to get one. You'll essentially be tried out to see if you're right for the job.

Sometimes you may be offered less money for a temp-to-permanent assignment since you could wind up with a job in the end, which coordinators know is worth a lot. Whether you haggle over this will depend on how much you want the job and how much competition you have. Don't forget that you're trying out the client company too. There's no commitment on either end.

WHAT'S YOUR BOTTOM RATE?

This is a question only you can answer. You know what you need to make and what you have earned in the past. And you know what your options are if you turn down an assignment. The important thing is to establish an absolute bottom rate in your mind and then never go below it unless you have no other options.

You may be asked if you would like to be called to consider assignments below your rate. It's up to you, of course, but once you go below your rate, you might find it's hard to get a rate you want if you work for a company that doesn't offer fixed rates.

I'll be discussing how to get rates up shortly. But what's most important during the interview process is being prepared to answer this question. If the coordinator doesn't bring it up, bring it up yourself. Be businesslike.

TEMPING TIP

If you're a professional or have a great deal of work experience and consider yourself way overqualified for the type of temporary work you're applying for, be mindful of your tone, your body language, and how you're presenting yourself. Don't let your tender ego prevent you from using temping as a stepping-stone to what you want. Coordinators are quite used to highly skilled and well-educated professionals working as temps. You won't be the first.

TIME FOR YOU, TOO, TO ASK QUESTIONS

The interview is also the time for you to ask questions of the temporary help company. Much of what you need to know about the company will be covered during the interview or in company handouts detailing insurance benefits, vacation policies, bonus pay, incentive programs, etc.

By the time you leave the office you should have been told the types of industries the temp company services, the usual length of assignment, the skills required, and any specifics unique to the company (malpractice insurance, nondisclosure pledges required, housing arrangements when you are assigned out of town, on-site training periods, etc.)

Since most of your questions will be answered during the interview or through company literature, there's no point in making a three-page list of questions to take with you. By the time you fill out the application, take the tests, and answer the coordinator's questions, you'll probably be too tired to go through another question-and-answer period anyway. You'll just want to get out of there and relax so you can have a chance to digest what you've learned.

Still, you don't want to leave without finding out what you really need to know. Your best bet is to concentrate on a few questions that will answer your one basic question: Is this going to work for me? The rest can wait. You can always call later about anything that puzzles you.

What is your objective? Are you going to try temping to find a full-time job, for example? If so, why waste your time and your coordinator's time with questions about bonuses or vacation? Concentrate on asking the coordinator questions like:

- What does the company have in the way of temp-to-permanent and long-term assignments?
- What kind of industry does the company primarily deal with, and what skills are needed to get inside those companies?
- What happens if someone wants to hire me?
- What courses do you recommend I take to improve my chances of getting into a good client company?
- Does the company offer any free computer classes to teach me skills that would help me in my career?

If a flexible schedule is your goal while you're raising children, now's not the time to be curious about the possibility of full-time job opportunities. Instead, ask:

- What are the chances of working from 7 A.M. until 3 P.M.?
- Are evening hours possible?
- Are there ever half-day assignments?
- What if my children are ill and I'm scheduled to work?

If you plan to temp because you're bored with your present job and heard you could make more money as a temp, the hours are not a priority for you. Rather, ask:

- Is my bottom rate reasonable and realistic?
- Will I get enough work to keep busy if I quit my present job?
- Will there be opportunities for me to advance?
- Will my rate stay the same or fluctuate from job to job?
- Are insurance benefits available if I need them?

FIVE WAYS TO AVOID COMMON MISTAKES ON AN INTERVIEW

1. Dress like a professional.

    This is a *real* interview. Temp help company coordinators need to know what kind of first impression you're going to make on assignments at their clients' corporations. They can't do that if you look like you've come straight from a cookout.

2. Act like you take the interview seriously.

    Don't adopt the attitude that temporary work isn't a real job, or you won't get a real paycheck.

3. Don't bring your children.

    You wouldn't bring them on a full-time job interview. It's just as unprofessional to bring them to a temporary help company interview.

4. Be prepared.

    Don't take a passive role by speaking only when spoken to. Have confidence in yourself and contribute to the process. You will be a representative of the company. Show your interest and your sparkling personality.

5. Be tactful.

    You want to learn as much as you can about the company, but don't fire questions at your interviewer as if you're conducting an investigation. Yes, you're shopping for a temp help company, but don't act as if you'll be doing the company a favor if you sign on.

    In short, behave exactly as you would on a interview for a full-time job. It could turn out to be one.

If you want to temp because you're reentering the job market and need experience but are a little (or very) nervous about going to work in strange places, you're not interested in advancement at the moment—survival is your goal. Discuss your concerns and give your coordinator a chance to reassure you. What if you arrive at the job and find yourself underqualified? What if you get lost on the way to an assignment? What if the boss is an ogre? These are all questions temporary help companies have dealt with before; your temp coordinator can give you answers.

TAKE THE INITIATIVE IN ASKING FOR ASSIGNMENTS

One of the biggest mistakes new temporary workers make is signing up at temporary help companies and then assuming their coordinators are going to start calling with assignments. They very well may—eventually—but you have to do more than wait by the phone.

Before you even leave the coordinator's office, make sure you've established how often and at what time(s) of day you will be welcome to call to see if work has come in, *even if the coordinator says someone will call you.*

If you're getting the message that the coordinator doesn't want you to call, you may not have the skills he or she is looking for. Or it could mean there is not enough work to justify frequent phone calls. Ask for the truth—in a pleasant way—and take it from there.

If you do get the message that you're welcome to call, ask exactly how often and what times are best. Then do it.

TEMPING TIP

Most temporary help coordinators expect you to be aggressive in going after assignments—it shows you're eager to work, which is a good sign.

Good coordinators who really can use your skills will advise you to bug them by calling in often. None of us like to bother people when it's obvious that they're busy, but this is one time when you can't afford to be too polite.

Some of the bigger companies have receptionists who do nothing but take calls from people looking for assignments. They don't care how often you call as long as you don't go to extremes; they're on the phone all day anyway. Of course, if a coordinator specifically tells you not to call until Friday, you shouldn't. You don't want to harass people.

"We're only human," says Pat Brie of J. R. Personnel/AID Temporary. "Quite frankly, it's impossible to remember everyone we have working for us. If a temp keeps calling in, eventually the name is going to stick. And calling in a lot tells me those temps are eager to work, so I'll put their cards first for an open job order.

"My advice to someone who wants to get assignments is: Be aggressive in a nonirritating way. Call in often but don't tie up the phone. Keep it short. Say something like 'Hi, this is Sue Jones just checking in.'"

AN ANSWERING MACHINE IS A MUST

While we're on the subject of phoning in, an answering machine that you can call for your messages is considered standard equipment if you're going to work as a temp. A coordinator needs to be able to reach you right away when jobs come in. You also need to supply the temporary help company with a phone number where you can be reached. If you're already on assignment, your coordinator can call you at your work site to run the next assignment by you.

However, if you're on assignment for another temp help company, it's not a good idea to give out your work number to anyone but your family (in case there's an emergency). For one thing, you shouldn't be receiving personal phone calls when you're working. Of course, everyone does, but clients especially frown on temporaries using the phone because they're apt to be paying a high hourly rate, they're usually under a time crunch, and they don't know you well enough to realize you wouldn't abuse phone privileges.

Secondly, if you're working for more than one temp company and the companies are fiercely competitive, it's best to keep where you're working to yourself and call the coordinator instead. In one worst-case scenario, if temp company B found out you were also signed up with temp company A, company B could offer your services to a client cheaper than company A, and company A would not be happy about that. It's a long shot, but why ask for trouble?

****

So much for avoiding awkward situations. Now that you know how to get started, you're ready to set your goals and choose your temp track—or tracks.

On the Job

There *is* no typical temporary assignment, which is precisely why a lot of people like temp work.

There are so many professions, so many fields, so many jobs, and so many work environments that I can't even come close to describing the typical temporary assignment. What I can do, though, in this chapter is give you a sampling of not-too-unusual office temping assignments—office work is as typical as temping gets. Of course, depending on your skills and training, your temp assignment could instead be in a hospital, clinic, laboratory, orchard, warehouse, factory, hotel, or nursing home. And if you're a graphic designer, word processor operator, or accountant, you're going to have an entirely different temporary work experience than a lab technician, nurse, or pharmacist in a hospital.

Still, the basic premise will be the same. If you plug in the variables pertinent to your own situation, much of the information I'm going to give you should still be applicable. As you read about what the first day on a new job might be like, I hope you can pick up a few pointers that will help you avoid mistakes others have made starting out. The more information you have about temporary work, after all, the easier it will be for you when you try it.

The following is a compilation of approaches to temporary work that have worked for me and many other temps I've compared notes with over the years.

ARRIVE EARLY

It may go without saying, but you can save yourself stress if, on the first day of a new assignment, you give yourself extra time in case you get lost. Once you've found the address, you can use any extra time to relax before you start work. If the workplace is already open for the day, you can inform the receptionist that you've arrived and then go back out, take some time to relax, get your bearings, and freshen up. I always bring a paperback or newspaper with me in case I'm really early and have time to kill. Don't kill time on the client's premises, though. Being seen lounging in the lobby doesn't make a positive first impression, even if you are on your own time.

DRESS FOR A GOOD FIRST IMPRESSION

Your agency coordinator will probably tell you to dress up for the first day on an assignment, and I think it's a good idea too, even if the place is informal. You'll feel more professional and make a good first impression, which will give you confidence.

PREPARING FOR THE FIRST DAY ON THE JOB

The last thing you need when you're hurrying to new assignment is to be shuffling through a stack of business cards or searching through your pockets for directions. When I'm temping I always record information I consider vital in my temping notebook. (See chapter 4 for more on keeping a notebook.) On the inside back cover, I tape all my recruiters' business cards so I can quickly find phone numbers if I need to call for additional directions. I also use these when I'm shopping around for my next assignment. On the inside front cover, I staple a small map of the city I'll be working in. Some temporary companies supply these maps; it's helpful to keep them handy. A reliable street map is also a good investment.

As soon as I'm scheduled for an assignment, I enter the information in my book, with the company name, the contact person's name, the name of the person I'll be working for, and his or her department, address, and phone number. I also record the hourly rate, the assignment length, and the name of the temp help company that got me the assignment. If you're using an appointment book and there's not enough space to write out directions, you can print them on a separate piece of paper and staple them to the same page. I also clip time cards and any temp help company pamphlets that describe the procedures I'm supposed to follow to get paid. These procedures differ from temp company to temp company.

GETTING ORIENTED

When you arrive at an assignment on the first day, a contact person will meet you and show you where you'll be working or, in the case of a long-term assignment, where you'll be training. In a big company or hospital, this person is often from the human resources department. In a smaller company it could be anyone—including the president.

REMEMBERING NAMES

Often your temp help company coordinator will tell you the names of the people you'll be working for before you arrive at the work site, and you'll have these written down so you'll know whom to ask for when you get there. If the names weren't available to the coordinator at the time you were given the assignment, ask your contact person to fill you in.

If your contact person starts rattling off a list of people you'll be working for as you're walking to your temporary desk, stop in your tracks, if you have to, and explain politely that you'd like to write this information down before you forget it.

As you jot down names, try to get correct spellings and titles. (I write these next to the date in my temping notebook.) You may need this information later for a variety of reasons. Don't be embarrassed. Your contact person will understand. It's hard to remember every detail while you're taking in your new surroundings, so write down as much as you can. Obviously, the name of your supervisor for the assignment is an important detail.

You will, of course, be introduced to everyone you'll be working with, but that's not the best time to haul out your notebook and jot down names with correct spellings. You'll be too busy smiling, being charming, and making a good first impression. Under these circumstances, it's understandable if you forget the supervisor's name and have to ask him or her to repeat it ten minutes after you've met—but wouldn't you rather avoid that if you can?

If you think back to your first day on most any job, you'll recall being so disoriented that you became exhausted from struggling to adjust. As a temp, you may experience such first days once a week or more, so you must learn to cope. And you will.

MAINTAINING A CONTACT LIST

Use your temping notebook to write down tasks you've completed, new equipment you've used, and the names of people who could become job contacts. Believe it or not, after a while you'll forget some of the places you've worked, the names of the people you've worked for, and even what you did there.

When you're looking for a job and see a position advertised in the paper, it's a big plus to be able to call or write the place and indicate that you've worked there before as a temp, listing names, departments, tasks, and dates. That way, all the human resources director has to do is call the person you once worked for and refresh his or her memory. You've got an instant reference. This obviously makes a much better impression than saying "I worked there a couple of years ago, although I can't recall the name of the person I worked for. He was kind of tall and had something to do with marketing."

I've also found that if you use your records to quickly refresh busy coordinators' memories about where you've worked for them before, you'll get assignments much faster than you would if they had to dig out your file, go through it, and call you back. Ten other temps could call in the meantime, and one of them could get the job. Coordinators can't remember everyone and where they worked. Help them out.

You'll also find this information useful when it comes time to update your resume. Instead of trying to recall names of companies you've worked for and the projects you worked on, you'll have a list.

FINDING YOUR BEARINGS

Big companies, hospitals, and factories can be mazelike. As you're led to your workstation, try to remember to look for landmarks so you'll be able to find your way around later. It will save you from having to ask for directions to the elevator or front door when it's time for lunch or when you need to find your contact person. Although there's nothing at all wrong with asking for directions, it always gives me the unpleasant feeling that I'm wearing a sign reading "temp," a feeling I assume you wouldn't enjoy either.

It wouldn't hurt to locate the stairs, either, in case the fire alarm goes off. People never think to show temps where the stairs or emergency exits are.

I recall a tense moment in an elevator after lunch one day, when I realized I had forgotten to note what floor I had been working on. Feeling ridiculous, I had to return to the lobby, find the directory, and hope I could remember the name of the law firm I was working for so I could pick it out from the other 50 firms listed. When you move from firm to firm on a weekly basis, strings of partners' names become hard to remember. (Was it Scribb, Jones, Taylor or Smith, Taylor, Jones?)

Chances are you'll be working for more than one person. There will be introductions all around, and then everyone will go back into their offices. It can be like a shell game trying to remember who went where and who's who.

How good are you at remembering names and faces? With any luck everyone's names will be on their office doors or desks, which will help tremendously, but you can't count on this. Make a "cheat sheet" to refer to.

PREPARING YOUR "CHEAT SHEET"

If there are a lot of people in the department you're working in and you can't remember who's who after you've met everyone, draw a quick map of the offices, labs, or whatever and then pick out the friendliest face you see and ask him or her to point out who is behind which door. Label your map accordingly. You might feel silly, but this information can save you lots of anxiety and confusion as the job progresses.

Use clues to help you put names and faces together. For example, under the appropriate door on your map write down Dr. George Jones, mustache; Professor Harold Smith, gray hair. If you must use uncomplimentary remarks to help you remember people ("dopey looking guy" or "lips like a duck"), use an indecipherable code in case your map falls into the wrong hands.

HANDLING NEW ASSIGNMENTS

Most people can put themselves in the place of a newcomer and will, therefore, patiently and methodically provide you with the information you need to get a job done. But there is invariably at least one person on every work assignment who will say something like "Hi, I'm George. When you're through with the spreadsheet [or lab report or proposal] you're working on, could you bring it to Stan with the Jasper account and tell him to sign the A form and then fax it to Joe at headquarters?" Then he'll dash off, leaving you to wonder, "Who's George? Where's the Jasper account? Who's Stan? Where's Stan? What A form? Where's the fax? How does it work? Who's Joe? Where's headquarters? What's the fax number?"

What would you do in a situation like this?

A. Get upset because you don't have enough information and call your coordinator or seek out your contact person and complain.

B. Ask someone near you to do the job for you since you don't understand what George meant.

C. Remain calm and tell yourself you can ask for help and no one will think less of you, but first see how much you can accomplish on your own.

One of the keys to being successful as a temp in any field is resourcefulness; in case you had any doubt, you should have answered C.

It's a good idea to do what you can before asking for help. In this particular situation you could:

1. Finish the spreadsheet.

2. Locate Stan's office on your map.

3. Look through your temporary desk files and vertical files to see if there's a folder marked "Jasper."

4. Take these materials to Stan and repeat your instructions as you understood them.

5. Ask Stan to provide you with the rest of the information you need to know (the fax number for headquarters, etc.).

6. Before faxing, follow up with George to be sure you completed the assignment correctly to this point. If you get stuck at any point, seek help. No big deal. Don't expect to be told everything you need to know to do a job—it rarely happens.

The first couple of times you go out on assignments, you may be so overwhelmed that a million "what ifs" about the job occur to you. You may begin to imagine everything that could possibly go wrong. This is natural when you're under stress, but you have to get a grip on your anxiety or you'll appear unequal to the job. Hide your nervousness well.

THINK FIRST, THEN ASK QUESTIONS

Of course, I don't mean that you should not ask important questions. You'll be expected to seek the information you need to do your job. But always think about when, how, and why you ask questions.

If you start on a task and need more information, take out your notebook and write your questions down—unless, that is, you need immediate answers to proceed. Let's say you're a graphic artist and need to find out if the company wants to use its logo on each page and what kind of typeface it prefers for the brochure you're designing. Can you make progress with the rest of the job? If you can, then you can show your supervisor results when he or she comes by to check on you before you proceed to ask the questions you've jotted down.

If you must ask a question before you can get started on a project, take a few minutes to look over the assignment, if that's possible, to see if there's anything else you're going to need to know to get the job done. Asking a series of questions all at once rather than one question after another shows you've analyzed the situation and are getting all the necessary information you need to proceed. It's also less disruptive to the people you'll be working for.

You have to use your own judgment about when to ask questions and when not to. You should not be sitting at your desk or workstation in a state of anxiety, stuck on a problem but afraid to appear stupid by asking for clarification. Neither should you be hopping up from your chair every few minutes interrupting people with unnecessary questions.

Consider that asking questions is sometimes a way for people to abdicate responsibility rather than get information. When people don't feel confident in what they're doing, for instance, they may ask other people to make decisions for them. Then, should anything go wrong, they can say, "Don't blame me. I was just following instructions."

TEMPING TIP

Instead of voicing each worry you have and appearing over-whelmed, calmly ask your contact person for the name, location, and phone number of someone you can consult if problems arise.

Remember that companies hire temporary workers because they want capable, quick-witted help in a hurry. They hope for someone who can come in, learn quickly what needs to be done, and do the job with a minimum of hand-holding. When clients have to answer constant, unnecessary questions, that's hand-holding. It's also hand-holding when clients have to make too many decisions about the way a job gets done.

I remember a temp assignment I had at a very prestigious and fast-paced Boston law office. Another temp and I were assigned to prepare legal documents for attorneys who were getting ready for court cases. My co-worker was very bright and thorough, but instead of skipping over words she couldn't make out in the hand-written notes on the documents, she'd constantly interrupt the attorneys and ask for clarification. When she was finally told, with quite a bit of irritation, to leave blanks where there were words she didn't understand, she started fixating on whether to change a section of the document she considered grammatically flawed.

Instead of changing the section and flagging the text for the attorney to check, she squinted at, talked about, and fretted over it for so long that by the time she finally decided to change it, there was no time left to finish the document before court went into session. Needless to say, she was soon history at that firm.

GET THE TOOLS YOU NEED TO DO THE JOB

People in client companies often don't know what materials you need in order to do the job they're asking you to do. You have to tell them. Do you need a calculator, template, procedures manual, style book, special markers, better lighting? It's up to you to make sure you're set up. You know what the tools of your trade are.

I know some temps who carry a briefcase with their own supplies rather than wait for personnel to scrounge around the office for extras. They save themselves a lot of frustration, and they avoid getting stuck with a calculator with buttons too small for their fingers or pens that leak or smudge, or being left without a software reference book to consult.

TEMPING TIP

When you're on an assignment and a question occurs to you, think of yourself as a consultant rather than a temp. If you were considered one of the best in your field and people paid top dollar for your expertise, how would you act? Would a consultant ask whether page one should be stapled rather than paper clipped to page two? Would a consultant ask whether a grammar or math error should be corrected? Of course not. Take on some responsibility and give yourself some status. Allow people to rely on you and your good judgment.

GET BACKGROUND ON THE CLIENT COMPANY

No matter what kind of work you do, it always helps to have background information about the company and the people who work there. You can ask for a pamphlet describing the company's product, an annual report, or a directory—anything that spells out the background of the company, what it does, and who's who. At the very least, knowing what the company does will give meaning to your assigned job.

On one assignment I had to use a desktop publishing system to prepare a manual about a clock, which I thought would be a real bore. Once I learned that the clock was going to be used to tell time in space, the project became much more interesting.

On another job I had to transcribe a doctor's notes—technical work that didn't mean much to me. I was getting bored with the project until I found out from hospital literature that the doctor was world renowned for his research on fatal diseases. He had, in fact, been responsible for saving many lives. The information I was transcribing was critically important. You can bet I paid more attention to my work after that.

I always find it helps to know who's who in the upper management of the company, too, especially if you want to return to an assignment. Then, should Jane or Joe Smith come by and ask for a favor, and you happen to know he or she is president of the company, you can act accordingly. Let's face it, you don't win points when the company president calls and you say something like "Jane who? Could you spell that last name please?"

GET ALL THE INFORMATION YOU NEED

Mary E. Willard of Charlotte, North Carolina, who worked as a clerical temp while studying to be a paralegal, also recommends that you ask if there are any company policies that may affect you or special operating instructions necessary to do your job. "One of my favorite 'horror' stories as a temp," she wrote in an article for *Tempdigest,* "is the one about the company that forgot to tell me the elevators were locked between 12 and 1 P.M. I never did get out of the building for lunch!"[19]

If you arrive at an assignment and don't find the information you need, and there is no one who seems to know, you've got to do a little investigating. Nancy O'Brien, training coordinator at Pinch Hitters, Inc., of Pittsburgh, says, "It is perfectly proper for you to 'go through' the desk of the person you are replacing. All things that are in the work environment should be related to the job. Usually, if someone keeps any personal materials, they label them as such. If they have personal things that are not labeled, they are taking the chance that those items will be disturbed. If you come across something that's clearly personal, just put it back, but don't feel guilty—the permanent person should have either known better or taken the personal things home."[20]

O'Brien's philosophy applies to any kind of temp who is placed in unfamiliar surroundings and expected to figure out the job as best he or she can. Contact people at client companies have often told me to feel free to look through the desk for anything I need, or the person whose desk I'm using will leave me a note to that effect. If not, be sure to ask permission. You may feel uncomfortable if someone walks into the room and there you are, a total stranger, looking through somebody's desk drawer or file cabinets without permission.

"Most people," O'Brien says, "are generous and helpful when they know you are new or temporary. However, use good judgment. Approach a person who isn't obviously frantically busy. Smile and introduce yourself, if you haven't already. Don't pester one person. Thank them and offer to help them if you ever can."[21]

BECOME FAMILIAR WITH THE EQUIPMENT

If you arrive on an assignment and are faced with equipment you've never used before, don't panic. You will learn to operate each machine the same way you learned to operate the equipment you do know how to use—by doing. Naturally I'm not talking about hospital respirators or sophisticated equipment that requires a whole course's worth of instruction, but rather basic office equipment such as phones, fax machines, copiers, calculators, and the like. Office equipment—computers and word processing packages in particular—does vary. Chances are someone will give you basic instructions, and you can figure out the rest by yourself. Even if there's no one to help you, most machines have instruction manuals you can learn from.

Don't be afraid to try unfamiliar equipment. None of it is impossibly difficult to master, and you're probably not going to break anything. In the case of computers, if you know the basics of one software package, you can probably learn the rest of it easily.

If the equipment should not be operated by someone who's unfamiliar with it, the client company is responsible for telling you that. If mistakes are likely to cause a disaster, the company should provide guidance.

TEMPING TIP

A warning for people who use computers or word processors: Although you're probably not going to break anything, you could erase someone's files if you're not careful. If you're working on a long, major document that someone has already put hours into, ask that a copy of it be made and put on a disk only you are going to use. Leave the original document intact elsewhere. If you acci- dentally delete a document, you'll feel better if it's yours and not theirs. (And so will they!) Plus it will be easier for the company to find what you've done after you're gone if it's on a disk with your name on it.

HOW NOT TO SOUND LIKE A TEMP

High on any client's wish list is a temp who doesn't sound like a temp to the client's customers. If you're required to interact with customers over the phone, the first thing you need to do is learn how to use the hold and transfer buttons. Politely put the customer on hold if you don't know the answer to a question; then ask some- one for the information. Although I am the first to praise and defend temporary workers as capable, intelligent, and resourceful, I also know that customers, clients, and patients can be uncomfort- able when talking to temps instead of the people they're used to dealing with. You can't blame them. If you call your doctor, lawyer, or chief supplier of a product you need to have to run your business and a stranger answers and responds with "Sorry, I don't know; I'm a temp," you might worry that this stranger doesn't really care about your needs. It's a good idea to keep that in mind if you find yourself answering phones.

PROFESSIONAL POINTERS

Make an extra effort to be helpful and reassuring by sounding as professional as you can on the phone. Here are a few pointers:

- Keep the name of the company and a list of people you're working for and their extension numbers taped next to the phone so you never blank out and forget where you are and who you're working for. (Talk about making callers uncomfortable!) It's very easy to blank out on the phone when you move about from assignment to assignment frequently. You'll probably only hesitate for a second before it comes back to you, but a second is too long. That's long enough for the caller to wonder what in the heck is going on.

■ Find out exactly what the company wants you to say when you answer the phone and write it out like a little script. It might sound silly, but this, too, is easy to forget. If I hadn't written down a greeting such as "Endocrinology lab, Dr. Higgensmithly's office" and kept it next to the phone, there's no telling what would have come out of my mouth as I tried to remember my little speech on one of my first assignments.

If your crib sheet isn't handy for some reason and you momentarily forget where you are and whose phone you're picking up, it's better to simply state your name than to hesitate too long trying to think of exactly what you're supposed to say. "Jane Jones speaking, how many I help you?" might not be what the caller is used to hearing, but at least he or she is not hearing total silence or a strange croaking sound.

■ Make sure you know how to operate the hold button on the phone. Never cover the mouthpiece of a phone in the mistaken belief that the customer can't hear you. Phones today are like microphones. They magnify sound a lot more than the old ones did. Customers will hear you even if you cover the mouthpiece or move it to arm's length. (I've seen this proved in tests.)

KEEP YOUR SENSE OF HUMOR

Let's face it, life does get ridiculous sometimes, and temping shows you slices of life many people will never see. If you can laugh at some of the circumstances you find yourself in, you'll enjoy yourself a lot more. At the very least, you'll have great stories to tell.

Bernice Kanner, who works for *New York* magazine, wrote a funny article about her "undercover" experiences as a temp and the bosses *du jour* she ran into. At one family-owned company that manufactures plus-size clothing near Times Square, she had an especially bad day, from the moment the receptionist announced "Your girl is here" over the paging system until she stepped out into the pouring rain after a day of directing dozens of incoming calls to 73 different phone lines.

"Here I am at the bottom of the barrel in the barrel on the bottom," she wrote. "My office is a rickety chair surrounded by fake wood paneling, Armstrong tiles, and people who have obviously never read Miss Manners."[22]

Temporary situations really can be funny, but they can also be rewarding, meaningful, educational, and fun. And the best part is that they're all *temporary*.

CHAPTER
6

How to Make the Temp Track Work for You

You'll be doing yourself a big favor if you map out a strategy for the temping you will be doing rather than just jump in with no goals in mind. It's too easy to let weeks, months, and even years slip by while you move from assignment to assignment, taking whatever comes your way. Set a course instead.

The temp track is actually not one track but many, each one leading to a goal or goals. Decide what you want to get out of temping and then figure out what track will best get you there. That's how to make temping best work for you.

In this chapter I'll explore some of the most common temping tracks. I'll explain how you can get on them and stay on them until you reach the goals you've set for yourself.

TEMPING WITHOUT GOALS

Looking back at my years as a temp, I realize that I did gain a great deal of experience and skills from temporary work, but not nearly as much as I could have if I'd used temping to its fullest potential. For me, temp work offered flexibility when I needed it, but I could have also spent my temping time building up skills and expertise in specialized fields.

Had I focused on assignments in medical fields, which I find satisfying, I could have used the experience in a number of ways. I might have built a background for work as a medical writer, used what I learned as a base for a certificate in an allied health field, checked out jobs I might be interested in someday, or developed expertise as a word processor specializing in medical fields.

As it turned out, I did build up expertise as a word processor in legal fields, but that happened purely by chance, because law firms use temps quite often. Since I don't happen to enjoy law or endless word processing, it was essentially a waste of some good opportunities. If you set goals, you can avoid wasting the time and opportunities that I did.

TEMPING TIP

"Write down the number one reason you're temping and refer to it often to guide your temping decisions. If you're writing a screenplay, for instance, and using temporary work to pay the bills, don't start temping so much that you're too tired to write when you get home. At that point, temporary work no longer works for you—you work for it." That's the advice of Susan Minzter, who owns a training and consulting company called Cooperative Concepts in Westfield, New Jersey, for people who want to discover how temping can work for them.[23]

Before you can put yourself on a temp track, you've got to determine what type of experience is going to be most useful to you so you can ask for assignments in appropriate fields. You may not always get the work you want, but you'll increase the odds if you state your preferences and at least know what you're looking for.

GOAL: GET A FULL-TIME JOB

Temp company coordinators are generally not in the business of helping people find full-time jobs. Neither are they in the business of helping client companies find full-time employees. A temp help coordinator's job is to match client companies with temporary workers. Period.

As all parties know (or should know), however, many client-employee matches *are* made through temp help companies. Mitchell S. Fromstein, chief executive of Manpower Inc., the biggest temp help company in the world, once pointed out in discussing the industry, "We are quietly responsible for the migration of one million people annually from temporary employment status to permanent employees."[24]

If you want a job, maneuver yourself into one. Here are a couple of ways temping can help you can do this:

TEMP-TO-PERMANENT

To dramatically increase the odds of finding a job in your field, you can ask your coordinator to place you in a company that's interested in a "temp-to-permanent" arrangement. As I noted in chapter 4, temp-to-permanent means you'll begin working for a company as a temp and then, after a month or so, if your supervisors like you and like your work, they'll hire you as a full-time employee. There are no guarantees you will be hired, but there's a strong possibility.

You (and perhaps even your coordinator) may not know when you're in a temp-to-permanent arrangement. Understandably, some companies would prefer to try out employees without letting them know that they are being considered for full-time work. Who wants to reject someone who doesn't work out if they don't have to? For that matter, who wants to know they were rejected?

TEMPING TIP

If you really want to know if you're being considered for a full-time position, try asking your contact at the client company. Even if you don't get a direct answer, you may be able to get a good idea from his or her unguarded response.

Remember: While the company is checking you out, you are also checking the company out. One of the pluses of temporary work is the chance for you to get to know future bosses and co-workers and maybe familiarize yourself with some of the work you'll be doing—before you make a commitment. If you don't like the people or hate the job, you're gone. You can move on and try another company as soon as the assignment is complete.

Actually, of course, you can quit after accepting a full-time job too, but that's not as easy as it sounds. Before you quit, you've got to find a new job, and it's hard to schedule interviews when you're already working, especially when you're new and can't easily get time off. Having to explain to your next potential employer why you quit your former job so soon isn't that easy either. He or she is bound to wonder if you're difficult to work with.

TEMPING TIP

Obviously, your coordinator will have to consider you a sure bet before you're sent on a temp-to-permanent assignment. You must also be perceived as someone seriously interested in a full-time job at the company you're being sent to. Although no commitment is involved, the expectation will be that you'll stay if the arrangement works. You are essentially working on a trial basis. By advertising the temporary position as temp-to-permanent, the client company is asking for an informal commitment.

GOING AFTER UNADVERTISED JOBS

A temporary assignment can be a great way to get inside companies and look around for some of those wonderful unadvertised jobs we're always hearing about. It may take you a while, and the opportunities will depend on the economy and the field you're in, but the odds are good that eventually you'll be offered full-time jobs while on temporary assignments. The question is, will they be jobs you want?

HELP YOUR TEMP HELP COORDINATOR MARKET YOUR SKILLS

You can improve your chances of finding the right job if you help your coordinator market your skills. Temp help coordinators are not experts in every field. You have to spell out what you can do and how your skills can be used. As long as you're tactful and don't come off sounding like you're telling the coordinator how to do his or her job, your input will be welcome.

TEMPING TIP

Some temp help companies now use computers to search for appropriate candidates, and others will have to follow suit to keep up with the competition. Since computers can now sort information in any number of specific ways, the more skills and details you have listed in the data bank, the more often your name is going to appear on the screen as a candidate for assignments. So make sure you supply specific details.

GETTING ASSIGNMENTS THAT COULD LEAD TO A JOB

After working in a college where I talked to many students looking for jobs, I know that in some parts of the country training in high-growth fields may still not be enough to land a good position. These days you need both knowledge *and* experience to beat out the competition.

People who don't have a great deal of experience can take temp or per diem assignments to get the experience needed to land a full-time job in their field—but first they have to get on the right assignment.

Lisa, an English and economics major with a degree from an Ivy League college in Boston, found only temporary work when she graduated. As she told the *Boston Globe,* it came as a shock and a great disappointment to her that she couldn't use any of the knowledge and skills she worked so hard at college to acquire. She's in exactly the same position as many talented, educated people these days.

Lisa's English skills can be valuable to many client companies, but she can't assume that temp help coordinators will know that she has technical writing, copywriting, proofreading, and editing skills—unless she tells them. In order to make sure they know all her strengths, Lisa could tactfully say to her coordinators, for example, "I thought, since I have proofreading, editing, and writing skills, that I'd be especially useful in a publishing company, although I'd also like to work in advertising or for a company with a big marketing or technical writing department."

If she is applying for clerical positions, which she should since she has no experience in her field, she could also point out that practically every company needs someone with grammar, spelling, and editing skills. To cover all her bases, she might also provide coordinators with a list of the fields and companies in the area that she knows could use her skills. (How does she get such information? She's got to do her homework.)

There's a good chance that eventually a publishing company within commuting distance is going to need temporary help. When that happens, if Lisa's been persistent enough, her coordinators will think of her—assuming she's been reliable, agreeable, and flexible during previous assignments.

What also might happen, if Lisa has been an impressive worker, is that her coordinators will call a few publishing companies to offer the services of an eager, reliable, agreeable, and flexible English major—who by now also has office skills and experience gained through temp work—if they need help in the future. This is more than a long shot. Aggressive temporary help companies often use people like Lisa to help market their services to potential client companies.

What kinds of companies and fields could you work in? You might find it helpful to make a list, not only to give to your coordinator but to help keep you on track, too. Use the yellow pages, trade magazines, occupation reference books, and the help wanted ads in newspapers to trigger ideas.

TEN QUESTIONS TO ASK YOURSELF WHEN SETTING GOALS

1. Which field do you want to build a career in?
2. Which related fields would be useful in building your career?
3. Which fields interest you for possible backup careers?
4. Which fields are growing? (The U.S. Department of Labor's publication Occupational Outlook Quarterly can help you here.)
5. Which fields are you curious about?
6. Which fields would provide you with meaningful work?
7. Which fields would be fun to work in?
8. In which companies and fields could you pick up useful skills?
9. In which companies and fields could you meet valuable job contacts?
10. Do your temp help coordinators know your preferences?

GOAL: GAIN EXPOSURE AND MAKE CONTACTS

Don't underestimate the value of getting your foot in the door of a company, even if you're brought on for assignments that are a little below your skill and knowledge levels. Those assignments offer you chances to meet people who can help you, chances to prove yourself, and chances for others to discover your higher skills.

SEIZING OPPORTUNITIES TO SHOW YOUR STUFF

Even if a permanent job offer doesn't come from such assignments, you're still gaining practical skills that you can bring to future temp work. This increases your chances of getting into companies where you might, in turn, get a chance to "volunteer" any higher skills you may have.

TEMPING TIP

If you're asked to do something you weren't hired for, you're supposed to notify your temp help company in case it wants to charge a higher rate for your higher skills. I recommend that you do this if you feel you are being taken advantage of, but not if you're filling downtime by "volunteering." You should be able to tell whether the client company is taking advantage of you—or if it's giving you a valuable opportunity to show your stuff.

I've "volunteered" my English skills by composing letters for people in offices in which I've worked and by editing and proofreading while on word processing assignments. These opportunities gave me a chance to "audition" for other than entry-level positions. I've also "volunteered" my word processing skills while on editorial assignments.

One reason I do this is that I prefer to keep busy during any downtime, but there are other advantages too. "Volunteering" earns you "points," which will help you land another assignment or possibly a full-time job. It's quite common for a client company that knows your background to give you a shot at something you say you're good at. Why not? You've already proved yourself.

WHEN NOT *TO WORK AT YOUR FIRST-CHOICE COMPANY*

There are times when working as a temp for your first-choice company may not be a good idea. Let me explain.

Say there's a company you'd like to impress; it's the best company in your field and might be someplace you'd like to work someday. Is a temporary assignment going to give you a chance to showcase your best skills? Or are you going to be using your "subskills"?

Think carefully about the first impression you'll be making. Are your potential employers going to see you as an expert they're delighted they could get at such a reasonable rate? Or is your level of expertise going to be overlooked because you are working below your capabilities?

These days, so many people are working as temps that most employers won't think twice about professionals working on lesser-skilled assignments—but, human nature being what it is, some will. If you have real concerns about how you'll be perceived at a company you hope to impress, you might be better off building up your resume elsewhere and applying at that company later, when you're an even stronger candidate. You may want to discuss the matter with your temp help coordinator, who might have a good feel for the company's hiring practices and use of temps, but you'll probably be the best judge of what's the right plan of action for you.

TEMPING TIP

If you're not on a temp track to find full-time employment, you can gain a great deal by working for a company that's considered to be on the cutting edge in your field, no matter what you do at the company. It could be a great education and could give you the chance to meet influential people, and your time there will look impressive on your resume.

GOAL: ADD TO YOUR EXPERIENCE

Have you had trouble finding a full-time job in a particular field even though you have experience in that field? You may find that your skills are in demand on a temporary basis, and this could open lots of doors for you. Although they're not in the career counseling business, some temp help companies will recommend courses to advance you in your field if they see you as a good candidate for temp work. And as a temp, you will be inside companies where unadvertised jobs may be posted or discussed. What's more, you'll be gaining a broader base of experience and more skills all the time.

DEVELOPING FUTURE BUSINESS CONTACTS

The temporary work industry is changing so fast that new issues come up every day. One of these is the trend for temps to recruit clients for their own future business—the business they plan to start as soon as they've amassed enough capital (which they're earning from temporary work!).

Exposure is one of the best rewards of temporary work. If you do an outstanding job, people will remember you. Keep in mind, though, that while you are an employee for a temp help company you are at the client company to work and not to hustle potential customers.

GOAL: STAY FLEXIBLE

Without a doubt, most people consider flexibility the number one advantage of temp work.

All temps, whether they're lawyers, secretaries, engineers, accountants, doctors, or industrial workers, have the wonderful luxury of saying, "Sorry, I'm not available [pick one] today, this week, this month, this summer. I've got to [pick one] be with my children during their summer school break, study for finals, take a trip, attend a seminar, write a book, star in a play, go on tour with a rock band, stop and smell the roses."

The amount of flexibility you get as a temp worker depends on the type of work you do. As a general rule, assignments requiring more skills are usually longer than entry-level assignments. People in medical fields have more options as far as what time of day they work and for how many hours, since most medical facilities operate around the clock. Office workers, meanwhile, have more flexibility in length of assignments—jobs can be as short as half a day.

FLEXIBILITY NOW WHILE INVESTING IN YOUR FUTURE

A large segment of temporary workers has always consisted of what the industry calls "reentry people." These are individuals who have been out of the work force for some time and are trying to ease back in. Often they are mothers of young children who see temping as an interim step until it's time to either resume or start their careers.

When you ask people in these situations what they're up to, they'll often say something like "Oh, I'm just temping for now. I'm taking a couple of courses at night, and in a couple of years, when the kids are a little older, I'd like to study to be a paralegal and work in a law office" (or study nursing, or continue building my marketing experience, or get into sales . . .).

Even if the only reason you're thinking about temporary work is that you want a flexible schedule for the time being, why not also keep an eye toward the future instead of putting your life on hold?

CHOOSE A PROMISING TEMPING FIELD

Let's say you have a vague idea that you'd like to go back to school to study for a new career when the kids are older. Since paralegal work is considered a hot career these days, let's imagine that you want to go into that field when the time comes.

In the meantime, why not try to use temporary work to get experience and exposure where paralegals work? Instead of taking what comes your way and bouncing from a manufacturing company to a television studio to an insurance company, see if your coordinator can get you into law offices whenever possible. While you're there, find out if you really want to be a paralegal by watching paralegals work every day. Talk to them. Tell them about your career aspirations and see if they offer advice. Most people want to help whenever they can, and you can pick up some useful tips and insights. Of course, this doesn't mean you should keep people from their work, and you shouldn't be neglecting yours. But there will be times (on the elevator, during lunch, at the copy machine) when you can strike up a conversation with a paralegal, even if he or she only has time to answer a couple of your questions.

If the opportunity to chat doesn't present itself—and it might not, since law offices are always very busy—see if you can make an appointment with a paralegal for a brief talk. You could say, for example, "I've been thinking about studying to become a paralegal, and I wonder if you might have a chance to tell me a little about it. I just have a couple of questions. If you don't have time, I understand. I know that you're busy."

You could spend years in school and never get a true picture of what it's really like to be a paralegal. Your instructors, and even guest lecturers in your class, aren't going to give you the real story. As a temp you get the chance to see for yourself what that career, or any other career for that matter, is really like.

If you can, try out different law offices with the future in mind. Do some mental job shopping so you'll know where you eventually want to work. Get to know people and make job contacts that you can follow up on when you have your degree. At the very least, by the time you get to school you'll already know more than most students in the class, and your studies will have more meaning since you've seen examples of what the instructor is talking about.

The same principle applies to every field. If you're thinking about a medical career, work in hospitals, clinics, and doctors' offices. If you want to get into marketing, try companies that have marketing departments. If you're thinking about sales, get into companies that sell products or services. All you have to do is keep stating your preferences to your temp help coordinator.

GOAL: DEVELOP A BACKUP CAREER

Another traditional segment of the temporary help service industry is made up of people who are not in mainstream careers—writers, singers, dancers, artists, actors, musicians, athletes, models, etc. Since I'm a part of this segment myself, I realize that temporary work is often merely a vehicle people use when they're trying to accomplish what's really important to them.

If you're using—or thinking of using—temping this way, you might just as well get yourself on a temp track in case you don't land the part, your art is discovered only after you're dead, you break your toe while dancing, or your record is not a hit. If you pick a backup field to concentrate on, you might end up with a good career that can keep you afloat in case your dreams don't come true. (I do hope they come true, though.)

If you're an artist, maybe graphic arts or desktop publishing would be of more interest to you than banking. If you're a writer or musician, maybe marketing or advertising would be more appealing than a law office. If you're a dancer or athlete, maybe a medical field would be a better match than finance. Pick a field and concentrate on it; you may be happy you did years from now.

If you're a writer or artist, you might decide to publish a children's book someday. Too bad you spent all your temp days in banks when you might have been learning the ropes and meeting people in publishing houses. If you're a musician, some day down the line you might decide to do some self-promotion and will kick yourself for ignoring stints in marketing and advertising. If you're a dancer or athlete, you might later decide to be a physical or occupational therapist, and you'll regret the time you spent working in insurance companies when you might have been in hospitals making contacts and learning about sports injuries.

Is it as easy as I'm making it sound to get into the kind of companies you want to work for? Can you just sign up with a temporary help company and expect to work in nothing by law offices? To find out, all you have to do is ask. If you want to concentrate on legal work, for instance, there may be legal temp help companies in your area. But whatever field you're interested in, finding temp work in that area depends on many variables, most notably who you are, what you can do, and how much temporary work is available in that field.

GOAL: GET USEFUL TRAINING OR RETRAINING

To build a larger pool of skilled temps, many temporary help companies, especially the bigger ones, offer training. This training can last a few hours, a couple of days, or, when self-paced tutorials are offered, as long as you want it to. It can be free, "worked off," or available only after you've worked for the company for a certain number of hours.

In specialized fields, tuition reimbursement is often offered for courses you take on your own. Some companies have their own schools and instructors. In "traditional" temporary fields, you can pick up training in telemarketing, machine transcription, accounting, or, most commonly, computers.

DON'T UNDERESTIMATE YOUR NEED FOR COMPUTER KNOW-HOW

One advantage young people have over older, more skilled and experienced people is that they've been brought up with computers and aren't afraid of them. Older workers and people who have been out of the work force for some time can be. I know because I've met many of them. When you consider how quickly computer use has accelerated in recent years (think of ATMs and touch-screen computers in shopping malls), you can imagine how behind the times and overwhelmed people who don't have computer skills feel.

Sandra Pesmen, a syndicated columnist who writes about the job market, recalls a well-educated man who had held high management positions at a huge company for 25 years yet knew nothing about how to operate a computer. "He told me he and the other executives would stand around at computer trade shows totally confused, each with a note from their secretaries telling them what to buy," she said. When, at age 55, this manager found himself out of a job and not ready to retire, he could no longer ignore the fact that he had no easily transferable skills. Pesmen told him to "march over to a temporary agency and get to work—learn some practical skills."

TEMPING TIP

Top on any expert's list of employment tips, whether you're looking for full-time or part-time work, is: Get computer training.

If you need to enter the computer age, you may have to take a series of computer courses to get up to speed in your field, but definitely take advantage of any training temporary help companies have to offer if it's appropriate for your skill level. You'll probably find that a temporary help company can be a comfortable place to be introduced to computers. Unlike a computer class, where there are 30 or so computer whizzes in the room, you'll find fewer people, if any, training with you. When a temp company offers self-paced tutorial programs, as is often the case, you can hunt and peck away at your own speed without anyone watching.

Manpower Inc. has trained 500,000 temporary and permanent office workers to operate every kind of hardware and software commonly used in business. Manpower president Mitchell S. Fromstein realized in 1981 that he either had to keep Manpower's work force up to date on the latest hardware and software or risk his company's obsolescence.[25]

He decided to start up an extensive computer training program called Skillware, which the company describes as a self-paced, user-friendly program that requires a minimum of time—usually under two days. The training, offered free of charge with "no strings attached," is done on the most popular software and hardware used today.

Many other temp help companies have also invested heavily in such training equipment and programs. Even if you're already computer literate, you may be able to acquire advanced skills from temp help companies or brush up on your rusty skills so you'll feel comfortable and ready to go when you arrive on assignments.

TEMPING TIP

Invest your time wisely. Study the ads in your local papers to see if the skills you'll be learning will be in demand. If you have existing computer skills, would you be better off building on those rather than learning the basics of a new program? Is there a "niche" company in your area that specializes in an advanced computer skill for which you already have the basic knowledge?

At the very least, it's important to appear up to date and knowledgeable about computers, whether you're applying for a full-time job or a temporary one. The last thing you want to do is seem resistant to change or to learning new things. It certainly wouldn't hurt, either, to gain a new skill, even if you use it only to enhance your resume. If you can use the skill on the job, though, you'll have a lot more options for both full-time and temp work.

FOUR QUESTIONS TO ASK ABOUT TRAINING

1. Is training available? If so, what kind and how much?
2. Is the training free? If not, or if it requires an employment commitment, is it worth it?
3. Will your base fee increase after you've completed the training? If not, are there courses you can take on your own that will help increase your rate?
4. What kind of instruction will be offered and where? Is it one-on-one or a tutorial? Some training programs are better than others. There are companies that simply offer to let

you practice on their computers, while others feature state-of-the-art training equipment.

When you're asking these questions, be tactful. The goal is to investigate, not alienate. (See chapter 4 for more on questions you should ask temp companies before signing up.)

THINK AHEAD

As you're planning your temping strategy, setting goals, and choosing the temp track, or tracks, most likely to get you to those goals, remember:

- Don't limit yourself to one goal if you can reach several at the same time.
- Focus on career or secondary career paths. Build expertise in one or a few fields if possible rather than wasting your time taking whatever assignments come your way. (Even if you have no plan to work in these fields right now, these days it's crucial to have a backup to your chosen career.)
- Don't assume you'll be temping for only a short time. It often doesn't turn out that way, and you could be missing opportunities while searching for the perfect job or meeting short-term needs.

Advanced Temping

If you stick with temporary work long enough, whether by choice or not, there will come a time when you're ready to move beyond mere survival. At this point, when you're comfortable in the routine and confident in your abilities as a temp, you will want to plan a strategy to advance and use temporary work to your fullest advantage.

Depending on the field you're in and the demand for your skills, advancement could mean:

- earning a better hourly rate
- negotiating for the job opportunities and assignments you want
- becoming more specialized as a temp
- learning how to keep the work coming
- moving ahead in your field
- enjoying benefits and perks
- becoming a "career temp"

GETTING YOUR RATE UP

One of the first things you'll want to think about when you get into advanced temping is your rate.

Most assignments available through temporary help companies offer an hourly pay scale that is equal to or higher than the same hourly rate paid to a permanent employee doing the same work in the same position. If this is not your experience after three to six months or so of temping and you've proved yourself an asset to the temp help company you work for, it's time to address this issue and find out if your rate can be increased. Realistically, it may not be possible. It will depend on:

- the demand for your skills
- the amount of work in your field
- the competition for temporary assignments
- the health of the economy in general and your field in particular
- what the client is willing to pay for your skills
- whether you're using your top skills on assignments
- your starting rate

SHOULD YOU EXPECT REGULAR INCREASES?

On full-time jobs you've had in the past, you may have done such a smashing job that you were often rewarded with promotions and raises. Or you may have come to expect a raise every year with your annual review. Since raises and promotions are often among a company's retention tools, some full-time employees expect to receive regular salary increases without having to ask for them.

Many temp help companies also have a very structured series of guaranteed pay increases for excellent job performance and seniority and will either give you regular raises or negotiate a raise for you with the client you're currently working for. But you can't always count on this. As a temp you should not necessarily expect a regular rate increase.

To state the obvious, as a temp you're temporary. You could take a full-time job tomorrow or decide to take an entire season off. You know it. Your company knows it. That's why even if you knock yourself out and win five new clients for your temp help company, you cannot assume that after three to six months or even a year your rate will automatically go up.

Many temp help companies do work hard at offering retention incentives because they have more jobs to fill than they have temps for. At other companies, temps outnumber assignments, and therefore keeping track of when someone is due for a raise is not a priority—assuming a raise is even a consideration. That's why you may sometimes have to *ask* for more money, not an easy task for most of us.

That said, in some ways getting a salary increase is easier when you're a temp than when you're working full time. After all, when you're full time and you don't get a raise, what are you going to do, quit? Full-time jobs are hard to come by, and employers know it. As a temp, though, you can go to another temp help company the same day. Unless you're working for a company that's providing you with full benefits, what have you got to lose?

This is one reason (and there are many others) why signing up with more than one temp help company is important, if it's possible and appropriate in your line of work. You've got to have other work options waiting in the wings in order to negotiate for a higher rate. Of course, it goes without saying that you must handle this negotiating process with skill and tact, just as you would when negotiating for an increase at a full-time job. But before you go to your mirror and start practicing your pitch for a raise, you've got to determine if it's really feasible.

TEMPING TIP

When you sign up with a temp help company, you can ask about the policy concerning increases, but I strongly caution you to do it with great tact. Coordinators say warning bells go off when applicants push for increases before they've even started working. Ask the question lightly—make it sound as if you're just curious. When in doubt, consider how you'd handle such a question in an interview for a full-time job.

CONSIDER THE TIMES

In tough economic times, getting a rate increase is a lot harder than it might otherwise be. A certain amount of realism is necessary. Still, there's a difference between being realistic and assuming your prospects for a raise are hopeless.

Keep in mind that the temp help company does not want to charge client companies more than the competition does, so if it's not getting large fees from clients, your raise will have to come from the company's profits. That's why you have to look at your job performance from a temp help company's point of view. When you do ask for a raise, will the company think you're worth it?

IS A RATE INCREASE FEASIBLE FOR YOU?

When you can say yes to a number of these questions, you're in a position to negotiate for a higher rate in most temp help fields:

- Have you been with the company for at least three months?
- Have you accepted most, if not all, assignments offered?
- Instead of sounding relieved to hear you've made it to a new assignment, do your coordinators seem to take it for granted that you'll arrive on time?
- Do you have all the work you can handle and have to turn down assignments?
- Have you been offered full-time jobs by client companies and made your coordinators aware of that fact?
- Do client companies often request you when they need temporary help?
- Has your coordinator sent you to new clients when he or she wants to win over new accounts?
- Have you learned new skills that now make you more valuable to the company?
- Have you been flexible, trying to accommodate your

coordinator and the client companies whenever possible?

- Do you appear to be so confident about your abilities that no assignment in your field seems too tough for you to tackle?
- Have you stuck out a tough assignment and let your coordinator know about it?
- Have you done your coordinator favors such as working with a client known for being difficult, working unusual or long hours, or traveling great distances to get to a job because no other temp had your skills?
- Do you dress and act like a professional, making the temp help company look good?
- Are you well liked at the client companies you work for?
- Have you established a good relationship with your coordinator?
- Are you cheerful and easy to get along with?
- Are you using high-level skills that client companies are willing to pay for?
- Are your skills in demand?

Here are the steps that I and other temps I know have used to negotiate a rate increase. They're meant as suggestions, not rules. Do what's most comfortable for you. We all have our own style in handling these situations.

STEP 1: DO SOME RESEARCH

Before you ask for a raise, you may want to call a few temp help companies you've interviewed with and ask the coordinator there if you can get a better rate than your present temp help company is paying you. Quickly tick off a few of the assignments you've completed, top clients you've worked for, and your top skills to refresh the coordinator's memory. In other words, be your own promoter. Sell your skills. If other companies will go higher, you have leverage with your current company. You'll also have somewhere to turn in case you get a negative response from your temp help company. If you aren't offered a better rate elsewhere, you'll at least know what your options are.

STEP 2: PLAN YOUR APPROACH

When asking for a raise, be pleasantly businesslike, not demanding or hostile. If you know you've been an asset to the company, have confidence in yourself. You should ask the question as if you know your coordinator likes you, appreciates your work, and would love to see you get a raise.

Spend some time appreciating yourself before you ask for more money. Think of your successes; remember any tough assignments you've stuck out or the times you went out of your way for your coordinator and client company.

I've driven in snow and ice storms to get to assignments; worked all day and into the night to complete a project; driven an hour to start a job at 7 A.M.; worked frantically to meet a deadline; given up holidays; put up with difficult people and accepted assignments no one else would take—all the time knowing I had the option to say no. Those are the kinds of things you should pat yourself on the back for and remember when asking for a raise.

STEP 3: STATE YOUR CASE

When the time is right, you can then say something along the lines of "I'd like to get my rate up, and I've been told by another temp help company that I can get [whatever it is] more an hour, but I'd prefer to stay with your company since I've built up seniority and I'm being requested by your clients. Do you think we could negotiate an increase?" Be prepared to state what you had in mind for a rate rather than wait to be made an offer. Also be ready to quickly tick off a few reasons why you think you deserve a raise:

- You're reliable. (Remember that snowstorm and all the other times you came through?)
- You've been requested by client companies.
- You get good ratings from client companies. (You won't see

the rating cards client companies might be asked to fill out to appraise your performance, but you can make this assumption from the feedback you receive or ask for.)

STEP 4: IF THEY SAY NO, PLAN FOR THE NEXT STEP

Of course, just because you ask for a raise doesn't mean you'll get one. If you're easily replaced, if client companies aren't asking for your services, and if there are more workers than there are jobs in your field, you can guess the response you'll get when you ask for more money: No.

If that happens, don't despair and don't argue. Instead, step up your efforts to add skills to your repertoire and perhaps sharpen skills you already have to become an expert in one area. Not only will you become indispensable to your current temp help company but you may then be able to sign up with specialized temp help companies as well (see chapter 8).

MAINTAINING YOUR RATE

At the very least, if you can't get a raise because times are tough and there are more workers than work, you should try to make sure your rate stays the same and does not keep dipping. This can happen because temp help companies negotiate rates with client companies, some of whom will not pay as much as others. The difference must be made up somewhere, and sometimes it's passed on to the temps at companies that don't offer flat rates. Should you accept an assignment with a lower rate? Not if you have other options.

The way to keep your rate from dipping, temp help coordinators have told me, is to state your rate and keep restating it. You may even have to resort to turning down a few assignments below your rate before coordinators understand that your rate is your rate. Period. Of course, they have the option of placing someone else in the assignment, and they very well may. If you're lucky, you'll have options, too—in the form of offers from other temp help companies.

Eventually you will be called only when an assignment is at

your rate, which is what you really want. The key is how good you are and how much competition there is. If you're really good, you will get plenty of assignments at your rate even if it means the temp help company takes less. It's simply a question of supply and demand.

EXCEPTIONS TO YOUR RULE

Having said that, you should think about what exceptions you want to make to this rule. If you really want to work on children's books, let's say, and your coordinator has an assignment in the children's book division of a publisher, but it's below your rate, you'll still want to hear about it, won't you? Opportunities like this do come along often in temporary work.

TEMPING TIP

Tell your coordinator under what conditions you'd go below your bottom rate. The idea is to be firm, not rigid. There are times when money is not the most important factor in an assignment.

When my local coordinators used to offer me assignments below my rate, I'd say, "Thank you for running the assignment by me, but I really can't afford to take less than my rate. If that's the only assignment you have, I'll make arrangements to work in the city with someone else this week. But let me know if something at my rate comes along."

Or, if I were working in the city, I might say, "I can get almost that much a lot closer to home, and I won't have to pay transportation costs. I really need to get $X for the assignment for it to be worth my while."

In both cases I was merely stating facts, which is what you should be doing when you get to this stage. I could afford to say no because I was getting better offers. I had proved myself to be worth the extra money when other, less expensive temps could have been placed instead.

Appraise your own situation and the market for your skills before you follow suit. If you bluff, you might find yourself without any work.

I was rarely offered an assignment *above* my rate, but it did happen when my skills were exactly suited to a job. If temp help companies know you have options, you might be offered incentives to take an assignment.

CHECKING ON YOUR OPTIONS

If you aren't sure you can find a better-paying assignment but want to check with another coordinator before you commit to a low-paying one (or to work you don't particularly like), you can say something along these lines: "If that's the only assignment you have, I'd like to check on other options before I commit. Can I call you right back?"

You'll be gambling. You could lose the assignment if the company has other people to call and won't wait for your answer. Sometimes it will wait a short time if you're good, but you won't know if that's the case.

If you're willing to take the risk that you'll find something better before the assignment is filled, you'll have to work fast. Quickly call your other coordinators and see what's available.

This is when the process can become a poker game. Do you tell the coordinator at the first company that you have another offer? Do you say what the rate is? It depends on the circumstances and how good you are at negotiating. There are no rules on this—it's something you'll just have to develop a feel for. No matter what you do, though, let your first coordinator know as soon as possible what your decision is.

Once again, I realize it's tricky to be on the phone calling temp help companies when you're working on a temporary assignment, but it can be done. Of course, you want to keep the conversations short and be as discreet as possible, but if you're in a situation where you can't quietly make a few phone calls, you can explain to your supervisor that you have to line up work but are willing to make up the time either at lunch, on any breaks, or after work if that's possible. I've never encountered a problem with arranging for future assignments as long as I was sensitive to the client's needs and expectations.

WATCH FOR NEGOTIATING OPPORTUNITIES

When you're starting out with a temp help company, whenever you do a favor for the company—taking on an exceptionally difficult client, traveling much farther than you want to, responding quickly to an emergency, working odd or long hours—don't be afraid to negotiate.

Say, for example, "I'd like to help you out if I can. Could you get me a better rate for the job?" If that's not possible, or you're pretty new with the company, you can say, "Sure I'll help you out. Do you think this will improve my chances for a raise later on?" If your goal is to get a job in a particular field, you might also ask for help with that. When you're asked to take a tough assignment, you could say, "I really would rather not take this assignment, but if it means you'll think of me the next time a job in a [law firm, bank, publishing house, etc.] comes up, I'll help you out."

There's a fine line between being overly assertive and not being assertive enough. Try to walk it.

Needless to say, you shouldn't constantly ask for favors or even ask at all until you've established a comfortable relationship with a temp help company. You always want to be seen as cooperative and willing to go the extra mile. If you're not flexible and are difficult to deal with, you might as well know right now: You're not going to get assignments.

WHEN YOU'VE REACHED YOUR RATE SCALE LIMIT

You should also be aware that there is often a ceiling on rate scales in temporary work. You'll start out on the lower end of the scale, which means your rate can climb somewhat, but if you reach the max early, you will go no further, no matter how good you are. Some companies may already be paying you their top rate and may not be able to afford to give you a raise even if they agree that you deserve one.

This happened to me. After a few years as a temp, I was getting the top rate for my skills and could go no higher at the two temporary help companies I was working for in the suburbs. (I did, however, continue to get increases in the companies I worked for in the city.) When I reached the max, I began working on a plan to get myself into the specialized temp help companies. I'll tell you more about how to do this in chapter 8.

To go beyond the pay scale limit, you will have to get more training or education and move into a better-paying field, reach a higher skill level, or learn a new job. Or, once again, if you've been working in the suburbs, you can usually earn significantly more money working in urban areas.

MORE POINTS ON MONEY

- If you are paid a fluctuating scale, say $10 to $15 an hour, you should be sure your bottom rate, not your top rate, goes up. You might never be offered a top-paying assignment.

- Sign up with a number of companies and compare rates. That way you can be assured that your coordinator is paying you what you're worth instead of pocketing what should be your full share of the client's money.

  Temp help coordinators will tell you not to discuss your rate with anyone, but they know temps do compare notes. Temp help companies are also competitive and realize that today's temps shop around and know how to negotiate. These are just two reasons why rates tend to be in line from company to company. If you're not getting the current rate for your skill and you've tried several temp help companies, reassess your qualifications.

- If you're offered a long-term assignment, ask about the policy regarding merit raises. If you're not going to get one and the assignment lasts many months or even a year, you might want to think carefully before you commit yourself. Are you getting a lot of work? Would you be missing out on a temp-to-permanent position if that's what you're looking for? Can you afford to say no? Only you can weigh the pros and cons.

Make carefully thought-out decisions instead of leaving your fate in a coordinator's hands.

■ If you learn new skills on a job, make sure your coordinator knows about them. Depending on what they are, they could boost your rate. At the very least, you must help your coordinator keep your skill file up to date. Each new skill could mean new assignments and better rates.

■ Notify your coordinator of any changes in your assignment. If you're asked to do more than what was originally agreed upon, you're expected to tell your coordinator, who may charge the client company more for your services and also get you a better rate.

MAKE THE MOST OF CLIENT COMPLIMENTS

When you become a pro as a temp, you'll start being appreciated out loud. When that happens, remember that you've earned it and that it's okay to take advantage of the compliments. Here are a few suggestions:

■ Remind a client who paid you a compliment that he or she can ask for you again.

■ Leave your name and company phone number on a card (or use a business card) for the client's desk directory. Above your name write "Temp Accountant" or "Temp Graphic Designer" in the event your name is forgotten.

■ Ask the client to repeat the compliment to your temp help company.

■ In your temping notebook, jot down the name of the person who paid you a compliment, the date, and the company, in case you ever apply for a full-time job there.

■ Brag to your coordinator. He or she wants and needs to hear this. You're the coordinator's "product." Humbleness doesn't help either one of you.

■ Tell your coordinator yourself that the client has invited you to come back when a new assignment comes up.

■ If appropriate, tactfully inquire about a full-time job reference from the client. If possible, get it in writing.

On this last point, proceed cautiously. Giving a reference is a big favor, and you don't want to put the client on the spot. If you've been on an assignment for only a week, it's usually not appropriate to ask for a reference. Six months is a different story. You can give the client an out by saying something like "I'm looking for a full-time job. Do you have a policy regarding how long you need to know temporary employees before you can recommend them?"

MOVING AHEAD IN YOUR FIELD

When there's a high demand for temps in your field and you've proved that you're a client-pleaser, it's going to be easy to advance. Temp help companies that can't fill all the orders they get for help will be constantly thinking up ways to keep you happily working and available when they need you.

One way coordinators can keep you happy is to watch over your career and help you to advance, which, of course, is in the temp help company's best interest as well. The higher you climb, the higher the rate you and your temp help company share.

One physical therapy assistant told me that even before she graduated from college she was getting offers in the mail for per diem work. And now that she's got a few assignments under her belt, she finds herself in the catbird seat. She's constantly being offered incentives to keep her happy and available for work.

If you're in a field where you find yourself on the outside looking in, though, you'll be the one thinking up ways to please your temp help company. Still, although it may be more difficult to advance in low-growth fields, it can be done. It happens every day.

Karen Frank was working as a temporary secretary in the marketing department of a small publishing house when everyone suddenly quit at once. "I just stepped in and finished setting up the book tours that were scheduled," she said. "Someone had to do it." The company was so grateful and impressed that it hired Karen full time, and shortly after that she was stolen by a bigger publisher. "Just be on the lookout for opportunity and take a chance when you see one," she advises. "Volunteer to do more than you're asked to do and you'll move up."

BENEFITS

One of the biggest concerns about temporary work is benefits. You may be under the impression, from various media stories, that there aren't any. Let me set the record straight.

It's absolutely true that, traditionally, one of the main reasons people have preferred full-time work to temping or working for themselves has been that most companies offered their regular employees very attractive benefits packages, while most temporary help companies offered only minimum benefits, if any. In the past, full-time workers in this country could count on comprehensive health and dental insurance policies, vacations every year, excellent retirement plans, and maybe a Christmas bonus.

But that's all changing today. Many full-time employers are cutting back on their benefits packages, while many temp help companies are adding to theirs.

There are no givens anymore. You can't assume that as a temp you won't receive a good benefits package, any more than you can assume that as a full-time worker you will. There is a wide range of benefits available to temporary workers, just as there is a wide range of benefits for full-time workers. You'll have to look into and shop around for the best package once you know you'll be temping for a while.

After 240 hours with a temp help company specializing in office support, I was eligible to buy into group health and life insurance, which, in addition to worker's comp, is something many temp help companies offer. Earned holidays and vacation days are also pretty standard after you've worked a certain number of hours for a company. The amount of time you have to invest in the company to take advantage of these benefits will vary from place to place. If you have skills in booming fields, you may be eligible for better benefits than you were receiving as a full-time employee.

I don't want to give the impression, however, that there are no problems getting benefits in the temporary help industry. For now, there still are. The main problem is that temps at the lower end of the pay scale (and that includes a lot of people) simply can't afford to pay for their own group health insurance when that's all that's offered. If they are not covered by another family member, they simply go without. This, along with the fact that there are often no sick days and there's no money coming in between assignments, is a major problem, especially now that more people are temping for longer periods and often not by choice.

A NATIONAL HEALTH PLAN IN OUR FUTURE?

As I write this, health insurance is a hot topic in this country. It's too early to predict what impact a national health plan would have on the temporary help service industry, or on any American industry for that matter. Certainly, not having to worry about paying for medical care would come as a great relief for those temps who have no coverage. It is also interesting to consider what would happen if those now staying in full-time jobs solely because of health insurance suddenly had other options.

Perhaps when you read this the proposed national health program will be a reality. In any event, as you advance as a temp, keep current on changes in temp help company benefits of all kinds by studying ads even after you're established and working all you want.

According to National Association of Temporary Services (NATS) spokesman Bruce Steinberg, "There is clearly a growing trend for temp help companies that offer specialized or highly skilled temporary employees to corporate clients to offer a full benefits package. For these firms, the benefits package is a recruitment and retention tool."[26]

NATS GROUP HEALTH INSURANCE

NATS offers a group medical insurance plan that temps may carry with them if they change temp help companies. Such coverage can be helpful to temps who work through more than one temp help company and find it difficult to accrue enough time with any one of them to be eligible for benefits.

BENEFITS AT MACTEMPS

MacTemps, a company based in Cambridge, Massachusetts, that specializes in placing Macintosh computer temps, made headlines after announcing in spring 1993 that it would offer comprehensive benefits unheard of in many segments of the industry. Considered a small company, with 20 offices in the U.S. and London, MacTemps said it would give full medical and dental coverage, long-term disability, paid vacations and holidays, plus a 401(k) retirement plan to temps who work for the company 2,000 hours or more a year. Temps who log a minimum of 1,500 hours annually would receive dental coverage, long-term disability insurance, paid holidays, and a one-week vacation bonus. Workers with a minimum of 1,000 hours would be eligible for the 401(k) plan.

"We're doing this because we want to attract the best temps and keep them," MacTemps president John Chuang told me. In Chuang's opinion, the best temps are people who are pros at Macintosh and Windows programs and who prefer to remain temps, earning $14 to $30 an hour, rather than work full time. "We want a core of career temps," he said, "who enjoy the variety and flexibility of working for a number of clients on a full-time basis as temporaries."

Chuang also feels the temporary service industry has a moral obligation to provide benefits. "As companies across the country downsize, there is an increase in the number of temps, and there is every indication that the trend is going to continue," he said. "This could mean grave social consequences as more full-time jobs are being replaced by temporary jobs."

PERKS

Some cold, dark, soaking wet day, how'd you like to take a limousine to work? Maybe a free trip to the Bahamas appeals to you more? Or a $90 gift certificate for a meal at a four-star restaurant? How about an extra $1,000 in your pocket?

This is a sampling of the perks offered to some star temps working in a range of fields. The more competitive the times and the field, the better the perks when you get to the advanced stage.

Usually the perks come after you've worked a certain number of hours with a company, but in the really competitive fields, such as medicine, you could get bonuses just for going on an interview or referring a friend. Traveling health professionals, such as speech and language pathologists, respiratory therapists, physical therapists, radiologic technicians, occupational therapists, physicians, and nurses, can earn points toward a luxury vacation or thousands of dollars in cash bonuses (see *Parting Words: Temping Temptations* at the end of the book).

True, the most lavish perks go to people in the medical and highly skilled professional fields since the demand there is high, but most other temp help companies also offer some incentives to work for them, such as bonuses and benefits.

When I had worked 1,000 hours as a word processing temp for one company, I earned six paid holidays and a week's salary, and I qualified for group health insurance.

Other perks temp help companies offered me included flowers on my birthday and secretary's day (nice when you're a stranger at a client company and you feel like no one cares much about you), that free limo ride to work I mentioned earlier, $50 for each friend I referred, a bonus for each new client company I referred, free passes for public transportation, eligibility for the credit union, workers' compensation coverage, a get-together lunch on Fridays for those temps who picked up their paychecks, three guaranteed pay raises a year, and the chance to win the "temp-of-the-month" title, which came with the choice of dinner for two, cash, or a gift.

On "professional" assignments for specialized temp help companies, I became eligible for similar benefits, plus attendance bonuses for completing all assignments in a certain amount of time and tuition reimbursement for job-related continuing education.

TEMPING TIP

Make sure you get the details on perks you've got coming to you. Some temp help companies will expect you to keep track of your own time and let them know when you're due for a bonus, raise, or vacation. Others do the computation for you.

Once I had just taken a full-time job when a large bonus check from a temp help company came in the mail. Since I had been getting assignments through more than one temp help company, I had lost track of the number of hours I'd worked for each one, which was a mistake. If the company had left the record-keeping up to me, I'd have missed out on nearly a week's bonus pay.

You will be given a packet of information when you register at temp help companies, or you can call ahead and ask to have information mailed to you. It's a good idea to look into various companies' benefits when you're starting out, but don't forget: Benefits and perks won't do you much good if you're not getting all the work you need. That comes first. All the promises of free trips and cash bonuses aren't nearly as valuable as a good coordinator who takes an interest in seeing that you're kept busy and happy with your work.

NICHE TEMPING

MacTemps is a good example of a niche temp help company. It has identified a very specific skill that businesses need on a temporary basis and supplies only temps who meet that particular need. In MacTemps' case, that niche is expertise on Macintosh computer equipment and, more recently, Windows software.

The difference between niche temping and specialized temping, which I'll look at in greater detail in chapter 8, is narrowness of focus. While a great many people would qualify as computer temps, only people who are experts at Macintosh computer equipment and Windows would be eligible to work for MacTemps.

Claim Net, with corporate headquarters in Irvine, California, is another example of a niche temp help company. In addition to insurance-trained clerical support, Claim Net's specialty is providing temporary claims adjustors who handle claims for workers' compensation; property/casualty; Longshore and Harbor Workers' Act; and group health.

People who work for Claim Net must be very experienced, general manager Betty Brittingham told me in an interview. "We hire only experienced claims specialists such as former claims managers, supervisors, or senior adjustors," she said.

THE PLUSES FOR CLIENT COMPANIES

The advantage to client companies is that they get exactly the type and amount of help they need, quickly. In one instance Claim Net sent five high-level temporary adjustors to a company to clean up its extensive computer files in a hurry. The temps reviewed 1,000 cases on a Saturday, and the company was back on track without any disruption by Monday morning.

THE PLUSES FOR TEMPS

The rewards for working as a temp in a niche field are great. Since her temporary claims adjustors generally receive a higher rate per hour than their full-time counterparts, Brittingham told me, many work less than 12 months a year yet still make a comfortable living. Plus they avoid a great deal of the stress that comes with a full-time job in a tough field.

TEMPING TIP

If you could qualify as a consultant in a particular field, you might want to look around for a niche temporary help company that can use your skills. Businesses today are using temps as they used to use consultants.

Check your industry magazines for niche temping opportunities. Consider that you might have to travel and that you will definitely be expected to keep current in your field, attending seminars and subscribing to industry news sources, just as a consultant would. Unlike a consultant, though, you won't have to worry about the details of marketing yourself, bill collecting, or bookkeeping. You can just call your coordinator when you want to work.

CAREER TEMPS

The idea of turning temporary work into a career has always been a subject of debate. The issue is not whether it's possible; it is. The real issue is: Is it wise to become a career temp?

Career temps have been around for many years. They're people who constantly turn down full-time job offers because they prefer the variety and flexibility temporary work offers. Until recently, concerns about career temping have centered on two issues: developing an unstable work history and working without benefits.

When career temps want to reenter the work force because they want medical insurance and the opportunity to plan for retirement, will they be allowed back in? From a human resources director's point of view, the hesitation to hire career temps stems not from whether they are qualified but whether they will stay with a full-time job.

For those career temps who aren't covered by a family member's benefits or who don't get some benefits from their temp help company, the worry is: Am I taking too much of a risk? What about lack of retirement benefits, sick days, vacation days, and holidays and the possibility of no work between assignments?

One legal temp help company owner in Boston told me he worries about career temps so much that he actually pushes them to take full-time jobs even though it means he loses great paralegals, lawyers, and legal secretaries. "We're a small company," he said. "It was tough getting through the recession, and I really can't afford insurance for my temps. When I see people turning down full-time jobs and staying too long with temporary work because they like it, I tell them, 'Enough is enough. You've got to take one of these full-time jobs. I don't want to worry about you.'"

LESS STIGMA ABOUT BEING A TEMP

Soon no one will even question why people have become career temps. It will be understood that if a person is not "core," meaning one of the remaining members of a staff cut to the bone, then he or she is "contingent," meaning temporary, part time, or an independent contractor. The stigma of being a temp will be long gone.

For what it's worth, before the number of temporary help workers jumped and it became commonplace to temp, I didn't find much resistance when I applied for full-time jobs. I had three good reasons why I had become serious about working full time after I had temped for so long:

1. I had been raising young children who were now old enough to be left alone more often.

2. My benefits had been covered in the past but no longer were.

3. I had been working on freelance projects that had now come to an end.

You do have to convince your new employer that you're serious about a commitment to the company when you decide to end your stint as a career temp, but with fewer full-time jobs being offered these days and so many people working on a contingent basis, it's quite possible that no one will even ask your reason for making the switch. Then again, if temp help companies begin to offer all the benefits full-time companies used to offer, you may never need a full-time job.

USING TEMP WORK AS A SAFETY NET

By the time you're an advanced temp, you will have learned the ropes of temping, made some good contacts, and built up your resume. In other words, you will have developed a work safety net that you can always use. People move in and out of temp work all the time.

This is not to say that you can take a full-time job and then a few years later pick up the phone, call your favorite temporary help company, and expect to get assignments the next day. You may find that your friendly coordinator isn't there anymore and that you'll have to reestablish yourself with the new people.

That's okay. Once you've learned the basics of temporary work—how to market yourself and sell your skills—you can easily start again. A few assignments later you'll be back in business.

HOW TO KEEP THE WORK COMING

One of the most important things to learn about temporary work is how to keep the assignments coming. Especially when you work mainly on short-term assignments, this takes a lot of time and effort. If you can't afford not to work, it can also be stressful at times. Are you prepared for the challenges as well as the rewards?

KEEP LOOKING FOR NEW TEMP MARKETS

Once again, the best way to keep the work coming is to sign up with as many temp help companies as possible—the general temp help companies as well as those that place temps with specialized skills, if that's appropriate in your situation (see chapter 8). Even when you're established as a temp, keep looking for new temp markets. This is an industry that's changing practically every day.

The more companies that are looking for assignments for you, the better the odds that you'll keep work coming in with no downtime. (Of course, for some people, free time between assignments is why they took temporary work in the first place—they look forward to the downtime.)

TEN WAYS TO STAY MARKETABLE AS A TEMP

1. Become computer literate as fast as you can if you're not already. Find out what specific skills are most in demand in your area. (Call and ask a few temp help companies or study newspaper ads.)

2. Update your computer skills continually. Take advanced courses in the most marketable programs once you know

what they are, in addition to any computer training your temp help company offers when you sign up.

3. Make studying employment trends a hobby. Read national news magazines, the U.S. Department of Labor's magazine *Occupational Outlook Quarterly,* and big-city newspapers.

4. Don't throw out college and adult education catalogs when you get them in the mail. Study them. See what types of job training courses colleges offer. Consider which courses would update your skills.

5. Visit a library as often as you can and look over the trade magazines. Your community college library should have a wide selection. Read the temp help company ads and find out what temp skills they're bragging about.

6. Strive for a positive attitude. Even if you have to work far below your capabilities and usual pay rate, take pride in your work. Be upbeat and forward-thinking. It will help you maintain your self-esteem, and people will enjoy working with you.

7. If you need retraining and can't afford college even with financial aid, consider a series of practical skills courses or a one-year certificate that will increase your marketability as a temp. Then you can add experience to your new skills and create backup work if you need it.

8. Keep up to date in your field. Attend seminars and talk to people who know what's going on in your field.

9. Write a new resume for temporary work that spells out specific skills, even if some of them are your lesser skills. Temps are matched to jobs by their skills, not just by their overall qualifications.

10. Present yourself as a professional. Even on a landscaping, construction, or moving assignment where you're expected to get dirty, looking neat matters.

IT'S UP TO YOU

The keys to getting steady temp work are the same no matter what your line of work. Basically, you've got to:

- be your own manager
- plan ahead
- be resourceful
- keep current in your field
- be a pro at what you do in every sense of the word

Like most temps, I learned the process of keeping myself in temporary work through trial and error. In the beginning, I relied on one temp help company and took whatever assignments were offered to me—typical for a new temp. Usually there was enough work to keep me busy with no downtime between assignments, but after spending a few anxious Friday afternoons because nothing was scheduled for the following Monday, I began taking a more aggressive approach.

Here are the methods I learned to use to make sure I always got plenty of assignments from both traditional temp help companies and those that specialize in filling editorial assignments. I've already mentioned some of them, but they're worth bringing up again:

- Establish a good relationship with your coordinators. You need coordinators who think of you and care whether you have work.
- Make sure your coordinators know where to find you when you're not working for them. If you're working for another temp help company, call in often.
- The first day on an assignment, ask your contact person for permission to use the phone to call your temp help company. Forewarn your contact that you may need to spend your lunch hour or break time on the phone, and assure him or her that you won't be calling on company time or making toll calls.
- If things are slow in your field, plan on spending a lot of

time toward the end of the week calling temp help companies. This means scheduling your lunch break at times when you know coordinators will be in their offices, as long as your client company has no objections. Plan on at least an hour for your lunch break on your "phone day," and don't schedule errands, appointments, or restaurant lunches for that day.

- Always know where the closest pay phone is for those times when you don't want to be seen using the client's phone. If you get a break during your workday, you might want to slip down to the lobby to call your temp help company, if possible, rather than look like you're using the client's phone too much.

- Be organized for your "phone day." Make sure you always carry all your temp help company phone numbers with you so you don't have to waste time calling information. As I explained back in chapter 5, I taped my coordinators' business cards to the back of my temping notebook for quick reference. (Business cards will also help you keep companies' and coordinators' names straight.)

- Make sure you've asked your coordinators when and how often you can call in and then phone often, especially toward the end of the week. Don't assume you will be called when an assignment comes in. You will have lots of competition from other temps who will be calling in aggressively looking for work. That's what you should do, too. Remember that if you don't call them, coordinators may not think of you or might assume you don't need a new assignment.

- Each temp help company will have different ideas about the best times for you to call. Iron this out in advance. If you're working from week to week, start calling your temp help company for the next week's work at least by Wednesday. If nothing comes in by Thursday, call another company.

- Consider a car phone or beeper. Many assignments come in at the last minute, perhaps while you're commuting home from work.

■ Think of a telephone answering machine as standard equipment that's vital to your job. Make sure yours has remote pickup so that you can call in to get your messages when you're not home.

■ If you can't afford downtime, it's best to take long-term assignments whenever you're given the choice.

■ Avoid assignments that are less than a week long if you need steady work, especially if the days are split up—say, Monday and Wednesday. You might be told that the gaps can be filled, but that's pretty hard to do. I always had plenty of work, but two- or three-day assignments inevitably meant at least one day's lost wages.

■ Always set up your next assignment before your current assignment ends. The earlier the better.

■ When you do take long-term assignments, remind your coordinator at least a week in advance that the assignment is coming to a close. Don't rely on him or her to keep track of when you need more work, even though good coordinators try to keep on top of these details.

■ Establish a nest egg that you can draw on if and when work is slow.

Eventually you won't have to stop and think about how to keep temporary work coming in—you'll know the routine and will have worked out your own method. Either that or you'll realize that you can't survive on temp work alone or don't want to put up with the insecurity of not knowing where your next paycheck is coming from.

That's when you go to plan B or plan C (a full-time job, retraining, two or more part-time jobs, one part-time job plus temp work—whatever makes the most sense to you). But in the meantime, while you're working on plan B or C, you'll have figured out the best way to keep yourself in temp work.

YOUR RIGHTS AS A TEMP

The temp help industry is so competitive these days, it's unlikely that a company is going to risk its reputation by doing something unethical. But I do recall, from years ago, one company owner who infuriated a number of temp workers with her unfair business practices. She's no longer in business, partly because her long-term temp workers bailed out on her when a new company came to town. Here's why:

- She was unable to find temps any work at all just when they had accumulated almost enough hours to be eligible for a week's vacation.
- To get a raise, even after years with her company, temps had to ask the client companies to speak to her for them.
- She'd never warn temps about difficult client bosses.
- She offered lower rates during slow times or on Friday afternoons when temps did not have other work options, yet she'd never raise rates when times were busy.
- It became known that client companies paid higher rates for her long-term temps, but these increases were not passed along to the temps.

As I said, this woman operated in the early days of the temp help industry in her area, when there was hardly any competition; people made up rules and guidelines as they went along. Today the industry has grown into a big, sophisticated business with more checks and balances.

WHERE TO CALL FOR HELP

If you believe you're being treated unfairly as a temporary worker, you can contact the following offices for advice:

- Your state's Fair Employment Practices Agency
- Your state's Commission for Human Rights

It's hard to say which office will be most helpful, since that depends on your specific complaint. You may be referred around a bit before you get to the person who can answer your question or help you with a problem.

Check the blue pages of your phone book for numbers and addresses of the offices closest to you. Keep in mind that the names of these offices will vary slightly from state to state.

- The U.S. Department of Labor
  200 Constitution Avenue, NW
  Washington, DC 20210
  (202) 523-9475

- The Equal Opportunity Commission National Office
  2401 E Street, NW
  Washington, DC 20507
  (202) 663-4264

The number for general federal information is 800-347-1997, if you think another agency might be able to help.

- National Association of Temporary Services (NATS)
  119 South Saint Asaph Street
  Alexandria, VA 22314
  (703) 546-6287

About 85 percent of all temp help companies belong to this national organization. Member companies have agreed to adhere to a code of ethics. You will usually see a NATS sign in the lobby of temp help companies if they are members.

- Your local Better Business Bureau

This will be a private number, most likely in the white pages of your phone book. Town or city hall officials might be able to help find this number for you if you have trouble locating it, or you can call your local representative.

REPORTING PROBLEMS TO YOUR TEMP HELP COMPANY

In the case of large temp help companies, unfair or unethical behavior can also be reported to the temp help company's chief executive officer, president, or owner. Just ask the company's receptionist for the address or phone number for headquarters and the name of the company president or CEO. In many cases, this is your best recourse, since management does care about the company's image and will most likely respond to your concern or complaint.

CHAPTER 8

Specialized Temping

Do you have specialized skills that might make you a more valuable temp? Earn you more money? Open up more work opportunities? Get you into more appealing companies where you could do more interesting work? You may have skills you take for granted and don't think of in terms of marketability. Or you might find that by taking only one course or perhaps even a couple of weeks' worth of intensive training, you can equip yourself with specialized skills.

There are great advantages to having specific skills that qualify you to sign up with a temp help company that specializes:

- The pay rate is usually higher. Clients using specialized temp help companies want expertise and expect to pay more for it.
- The odds of getting into (or back into) an industry or company in your field are greater if you work for a specialized temp help company that focuses on your field rather than one that focuses on many fields.
- You can often climb more rapidly in your career by increasing your contacts and broadening your job experience through specialized temp help companies than by staying for years in a full-time job.

What's the catch? You've got to be very good at what you do, and you've got to know which of your skills you can best put to use in which fields.

THE HIDDEN JOB MARKET

You may be surprised to learn that even if you don't have advanced skills or any special training, there may still be a place for you. You've just got to uncover those hidden work opportunities.

While it's true that some companies recruit only cream-of-the-crop professionals in specific fields, there are others that look for people to fill a wide range of temporary jobs, from entry-level to highly advanced, so they can offer "package deals"—every skill a company needs for a project.

A good example of an entry-level job in a specialized field (in this case the legal field) is what Tom Routhier calls a "fax runner." Routhier, president of Routhier Placement Specialists in Boston, a temp help company that specializes in placing legal personnel, explains that a fax runner is just what the title indicates—someone who spends the entire day delivering the never-ending faxes sent to lawyers at giant law firms. Obviously, for a job like this no legal background is required.

Assess your skills with specialized temp help companies in mind. Look in the help wanted ads for your area. Then dig deeper and call.

If you don't have the primary skills a specialized company or division of a larger corporation offers to its clients (a law degree for work in a legal temp help company, or a science degree for a science temp help company, for instance), you can still break into specialized companies that provide a full range of temps. But you will have to have something special to offer, such as experience in the field or super skills and a great track record.

I broke into a legal temp help company after putting together a letter explaining my legal experience as a clerical temp and listing the law firms I had temped for, adding a reference from a lawyer. I could have made the same pitch on the phone, but putting it in writing meant it could be passed on through appropriate channels and put into an active file or database.

When I wanted to break into medical temp help companies that provided clerical workers in addition to medical professionals, I took a course in medical terminology so I could work as a word processing secretary in medical fields. The course was all I needed to pass the test I was given on medical terminology when I applied. And, coupled with my experience in hospitals, the course got me high paying, interesting assignments.

You might think taking a course or two is putting a lot of effort into temporary work, but this is the kind of energy and determination you should bring to temporary work today, especially if you don't have high-level skills or experience but want to advance and make good money. In my case, the investment was well worth the effort. By specializing, I could make up to $5 more an hour.

TEMPING TIP

Believe it—temping is here to stay. If you get into it, you may find it's not as temporary as you thought it would be. Put the emphasis on work, *not* temporary. *It's important to take temp work seriously these days and put as much effort into it as you would in going after a full-time job. It might just* become *your full-time job.*

Here are some steps you can take if you want to break into a specialized temp help field:

1. Decide what field you'd like to get into. Law? Medicine? Computers? Science? Accounting? Assess your skills with specialized temp help companies or specialized divisions of nonspecialized temp help companies in mind. Do you have anything to offer them? There's no harm in simply asking temp companies that specialize in your chosen field about your chances of getting work with them. Your burning desire to break into a field may be all it takes to become a candidate

for an entry-level position. Client companies and temp help companies love enthusiastic, eager-to-please temps.

2. Go through nonspecialized temp help companies and try for temporary jobs in the field you want to break into in order to build up your experience. This could take a while, even a year or more if you have no experience at all, but at least you'll be on your chosen temp track.

3. Try to get recommendations from people in the field while on temporary assignments.

4. Take courses to improve your chances of breaking into specialized fields. You may get advice on what courses to take by calling some temp help companies and asking about the basic requirements for temps they place.

5. If you don't have computer training, get it! If you have good computer skills—if, for example, you know how to work with spreadsheets, can use desktop publishing software, or have strong word processing skills—you'll have an easier time of breaking into specialized temp help companies.

Keep in mind that you can also break into specialized fields without going through a specialized temp help company. Many of the temp help companies that place a full range of temporary help can get you the same rates and number of assignments as specialized companies can.

This advice also applies if you do have top-flight skills. Many of the big companies that you might associate with traditional temp assignments like clerical and light industrial work are branching out and placing high-level professionals in a variety of fields. Some are also opening new divisions that concentrate in specialized areas to better service the growing and diverse needs of business.

You should also be aware that your skills might be valued at more than one type of specialized temporary help company, even though you might not associate your skills with the fields some of these companies specialize in.

You may think, for instance, that temporary help companies that specialize in technical fields place engineers and drafters. They do, but some also place plumbers, welders, electricians, salespeople, inspectors, technical writers, clerical workers, telemarketers, and computer pros.

Biotech is a booming industry at the moment, and you'd be right if you guessed that science temp help companies are doing a great business there. But if you look closer, you'll see that biotech companies also need legal professionals to help with patents, contracts, and other legal matters; accountants to handle tax and bookkeeping details; financial services people to handle investments; benefits experts to handle personnel issues; clerical support to handle paperwork; and computer professionals for lab work—in short, all the kinds of workers that make a booming business run smoothly.

What's your background? People in banking and finance can find work through temp help companies that specialize in accounting fields. Computer professionals can find work through companies specializing in medical, technical, clerical, and accounting fields, just to name a few, and clerical workers can find work through these same companies.

As a general rule, don't dismiss any temp help company as a possible source of work without first checking out its needs.

TEMPING TIP

Make it a habit to study the help wanted ads in your local newspapers every week, but don't seek out only the temp help companies that you know use your skills. Look at all the ads for temporary help. You might spot hidden markets for your skills. Help wanted ads are an education in themselves.

KEEP YOUR SPECIALIZED SKILLS CURRENT

If you decide to use your specialized skills for temping, be aware of a potential problem: skills slippage. "A temp's skill level can diminish considerably after leaving a permanent job," Amy Norton Paterson told me. She's the owner of Mortage Bankers'

Consultants in Dallas/Fort Worth, a company that specializes in placing finance professionals.

"Although part of the attraction of working as a temporary is that skills can be kept current, this will not happen if the temp works below his or her skill level. I've avoided this problem with the temps I place by reimbursing them for continuing education classes they take at a local college."[27]

If you're not being challenged as a temp and your skill level begins to slide, it's time to reassess. Think about these questions:

- Would you learn more and stay sharper in another field?
- Would further training improve your chances of getting more challenging assignments?
- Would another temp help company offer more advanced assignments?
- Is your coordinator pigeonholing you because he or she knows you do a great job on one particular kind of assignment?
- Is your coordinator clear on the kind of assignments you're capable of handling?

If you find you can't improve the skill level of the temp assignments you're getting, maybe temping's not for you, at least not as your sole means of support. Are there alternatives? Could you start your own consulting business? Could you take a challenging part-time job and augment it with temp work or your own freelance work? As long as you know you can always temp if you have to and have emergency money saved, you might want to experiment rather than stagnate.

The following is a sampling of the many specialized fields that hire temps. I hope they will spark your imagination and send you on your own search for temp help opportunities in your field.

TECHNICAL TEMPS

"We're spending a lot more time on the phone reeducating people about temporary work," said Rick Kehoe, who's in the sales and recruiting division of TAD Technical Services.

"We're seeing what we call nontraditional jobbers—people who have never temped before; people who have been laid off from jobs in technical fields that they've had for 15 to 20 years. They think that age is a deterrent to finding work, but we tell them that's not so; age is a benefit. By using older workers, client companies are starting to realize that they can get highly skilled people with a great deal of experience to work for them on a temporary basis.

"When we hear of companies laying off, we send out job postings to those companies to let people there know there's work in their field on a temporary basis."

Headquartered in Cambridge, Massachusetts, TAD Technical Services, which has over 200 companies nationwide and several overseas branches, has become so diversified, Kehoe explained, that the company now has four separate divisions: technical, accounting, clerical, and computer software.

TECHNICAL TEMPS

Temps needed include computer programmers, computer systems analysts, designers, drafters, editors, engineers, illustrators, licensed plumbers, welders, tech writers, proposal writers, CRD/CRM and AutoCad personnel, and customer service reps.

"When you're applying for full-time work you can elaborate on your skills at the interview, but you don't get that chance with clients when you're a temp. We send them your resume, so make sure it lists all your skills," said Kehoe. "Clients will call me and say, 'I can't tell by this person's resume if he has the specific skills needed for this particular job.' If this client has a stack of resumes to look over and one of the resumes lists each and every skill needed to get this client's job done, the client will look no further; he's found who he's looking for."

TEMPING TIP

Write a new resume just for temporary work. Make sure it spells out exactly the skills that you have and the equipment you're familiar with.

PROFESSIONAL TEMPS

Professional temp is a slippery term; it's hard to get a grip on what it means. (We're all professionals when we temp, after all.) Nevertheless, it's a widely used term and a popular topic of conversation. Usually it means a highly skilled, highly educated person who's using his or her skills in temporary work.

The National Association of Temporary Services (NATS) considers all of the following to be professional temps: accountants, auditors, CFOs (chief financial officers), paralegals, attorneys, designers, drafters, editors, engineers, and illustrators—but this is obviously just a sampling of occupations; there are many others.

It's impossible to cover all professional temp occupations here or even to identify them in any list. So consider the following just representative of trends in the industry. It should suggest possibilities open to professionals of all types today.

It's important to note that, despite all the national publicity about professional temps, which tends to play up the most interesting trends (CEOs and human resources pros temping, etc.), this segment of the industry is still relatively small.

As I write this, NATS estimates the number of professionals or other highly skilled workers at about 25 percent of the 1.15 million people who work as temps. In 1981 it was 14 percent. Office and clerical temps are still the mainstay of the industry, with industrial and technical temps following.

Despite the relatively small numbers, the future looks promising for professional temps. *Working Woman* magazine included professional temp placement on its list of the 25 hottest careers today in its July 1993 issue. From 1989 to 1991, the magazine reports, payroll for professional temp placement increased 12 percent—four times the increase of other temporary placement.[28]

Some professional temps have all the work they want and are so happy with their newfound freedom that they have no intention of going back to work full time. Ever. Others find it very tough to come up with enough assignments in their field and, if they're out of work, are using both their "professional" skills and "subskills" in hopes of getting inside companies and finding permanent work.

EXECUTIVE TEMPS

For superskilled executives—CEOs, COOs (chief operating officers), CFOs, or human resources, communications, or telecommunications pros—there is a growing but narrow market for short-term assignments through temporary help companies that specialize in placing executive temps.

According to David Lord, editor of *Executive Recruiter News,* executive temp companies together have 140 offices in North America and Europe and earn over $100 million in the U.S. alone.

EXECUTIVE TEMPS

Temps needed include specialists in stocks and bonds, law, accounting, finance, transportation, logistics and materials management, banking, marketing, programming, public relations, domestic and international entertainment, real estate, environment, chemical automation, communications and telecommunications systems, defense industries, publishing, crisis management, human resources, engineering, pharmaceutical and medical device companies, and mining.

WHO ARE EXECUTIVE TEMPS?

"[They are] recycled retirees, job hunters, lifestyle seekers, or refugees from the corporate routine, managers-turned-mothers, and career interim executives," Lord reported. "They are in between projects, unemployed, or self-employed. They are prescreened, high-level professionals often earning more than $100,000 who are no longer saddled with a stigma about temporary work."

WHY ARE EXECUTIVE TEMPS HIRED?

A CEO might be called in to help a company facing Chapter 11. A human resources pro might be hired when a company has to implement an entirely new benefits program. Assignments can last three months or as long as a year and typically run six to nine months.

While working as a temp executive might sound appealing, candidates must be realistic. The opportunities for such assignments are scarce. Hundreds and sometimes thousands of candidates may be available on executive temp databases for what might be only a relatively small number of assignments.

"The odds are long and the work is short-lived, but talented people who do make the grade sometimes end up with a permanent job if they want one," said Lord. He estimated that nationwide at least 15 percent of such executive temps wind up with full-time jobs, and he knows of one exec temp company that claims a 75 to 80 percent permanent placement rate.[29]

Of course, the pay rate varies and depends on the executive's "worth" and the client company's need for a certain skill. If the demand for some particular expertise is great, the exec temp firm can charge more. In general, Lord said, exec temp firms charge less than an independent consultant will for similar work, and this explains the growth in the use of exec temps. However, he added, "salaries are usually high enough to make some allowance for the fact that the work is temporary."

WHO USES EXECUTIVE TEMPS?

The *New York Times,* which dubbed high-level executives "elite temps" in a May 1993 article, cited household names like Johnson & Johnson, Walt Disney, I.B.M., Ford, and Fidelity Investments among the many companies now using "elite temps."[30]

One company chairman said a few years ago that he paid $2,250 a day to an executive temp firm for an engineer to assist in corporate development. The engineer, who had a doctorate in applied mathematics and once worked for an Air Force electronics think tank, got $1,500 a day, with an additional $750 a day going to the exec temp firm that placed him. It's very expensive, the chairman admitted, but "if we get what we want it will be more than worth it."[31]

SIGNING UP AS AN EXEC TEMP

If you qualify as an executive temp candidate, you can call exec temp placement firms to ask for an application to send back with your resume. If your skills are appropriate, your name and qualifications will be added to the firm's database. You will be called if an assignment comes in that matches your skills. There is usually no fee for being listed in the database, but you shouldn't expect a reply, and telephoning for information is discouraged. Firms have been getting a flood of resumes from job-hunting executives ever since the recent recession. Many executive temp placement companies also offer executive job searches and recruiting services.

To find executive temp placement firms to contact, study the trade magazines, newspapers, or newsletters that cover your field. Look for terms such as executive temporary, interim manager, flexible executive, contract professional, or line consultant. They all mean the same thing—highly skilled business professionals.

You can also send for the *Executive Recruiter News Directory of Executive Temporary Placement Firms,* which is available from Kennedy Publications. (See the appendix for more information.)

MEDICAL TEMPS

Without a doubt, the medical segment of the temporary help industry is booming and has been for some time. For physicians, locum tenens work (the term used for medical temping) is very attractive. They can avoid 24-hour days, heavy patient loads, and the stress that goes with them; costly malpractice insurance; and the headaches of running their own office.

Age is not a factor. Older physicians might be of retirement age yet reluctant to give up medicine completely. Residents might see temping as a way to get more varied experience in different settings. Some find more meaning in practicing where they're needed and using their specialized skills more often.

Another popular reason for doctors to do locum tenens work is the opportunity to travel both throughout the U.S. and abroad, although some locum tenens companies don't handle overseas travel because of the red tape involved.

MEDICAL TEMPS

Temps needed include nurses, physicians, respiratory and physical therapists and assistants, phlebotomists, maternal-child personnel, home health aids, elder companions, medical secretaries, pharmacists, transcriptionists, radiology technicians, medical assistants, laboratory technologists, medical billers, unit coordinators, certified nurse midwives, certified registered nurse anesthetists, cytotechnologists, physician assistants, nurse practitioners, speech-language pathologists, dosimetrists, and radiation therapists.

If you have medical skills, you can use them in many ways as a temp. You might find yourself on a plane headed across the country to help a disaster relief effort after a hurricane, flood, tornado, earthquake, fire, or riot—or you might be asked to assist some of the thousands of people who run the grueling Boston Marathon. You might be part of the supplemental staffing for hospitals, nursing homes, outpatient clinics, etc., or just work a few hours here and there to pick up extra cash. You can travel extensively (as you'll read about in more detail in *Parting Words: Temping Temptations* at the end of the book) or be placed locally. Or you can join a hospital's in-house pool of medical temps and work a schedule that suits you.

TEMPING TIP

People in the business say that since there are no strict regulations governing locum tenens firms, some are better than others. Do some comparison shopping and ask for references from your colleagues. Look for firms that do extensive reference checks and screening of your skills. If the company is thorough in checking you out, it will be thorough in checking out assignments too.

If you have medical skills or are planning to get some, the American Medical Association has a publication called *Guide to Locum Tenens Recruitment* that lists locum tenens firms and covers some of the basics. (See the appendix for details.)

LEGAL TEMPS

While the idea of using attorneys on a temporary basis is catching on, especially in major cities, the increase in the use of paralegals as temps has been the most startling change in this field. In fact, there is so much work for paralegals that many job-hunting lawyers are learning paralegal skills so they, too, can get their foot in the door of law firms.

Judith Serio, president of the Atlanta-based company Lawstaf, told me that although she places contract attorneys, legal secretaries, and receptionists, 75 percent of her temporary assignments go to paralegals, who end up taking full-time jobs about 20 percent of the time.

"I sent 90 paralegals to one project where they coded literally millions of documents," she explained. "They were like an army of paralegals walking into the firm. Of course, that's the extreme. The average is 20 to 30 per project. Usually they're called in when a major corporate case is going on and there are years' worth of documents to go over, looking for evidence. Sometimes so many paralegals go on an assignment together that they have to work in a warehouse or in some facility the firm rents."

LEGAL TEMPS

Temps needed include paralegals, attorneys, law clerks, coders, law office administrators and managers, law researchers, law librarians, litigation summary support people, legal writers, litigation support teams, investigators, and court reporters.

In her book, *Paralegal* (Peterson's, 1993), Barbara Bernardo notes, "While paralegal employment agencies offer permanent and temporary placement services, temporary assignments are an excellent way to obtain your first paralegal job. They give you the opportunity to gain valuable experience and test the waters before jumping in head first. Temping enables you to work at several different law firms or corporations before deciding what's best for you. And organizations often offer permanent positions to temporary workers. . . ."[32]

One advantage of working as a temporary lawyer, Judith Serio told me, is that temp lawyers may work 60 hours a week, just as an attorney from the firm will, but the temp gets paid for every single hour, while the firm's attorney just gets a straight salary. For those attorneys who wake up on Sunday morning with a full day's work ahead of them after already putting in a 60-hour week, getting paid an hourly rate can be very attractive.

If you don't have formal legal training, one way to get assignments with law firms is by looking for temporary word processing jobs, especially if you have high-speed keyboarding skills. The smaller firms in particular may be interested in you because they often don't want to pay a higher fee for a legal secretary when they only need a fast word processor operator.

Attorneys leave a very thorough paper trail, dictating volumes of information that have to be word processed. Temp help companies that specialize in legal personnel usually require their temps to have at least a year's experience in a law firm before they'll send them to even an entry-level assignment. After all, since they're paying a little more for temps with special skills, client companies expect them to sit down and start producing with very little instruction.

TEMPING TIP

To improve your chances of breaking into law firms as a temp word processor, take a course in legal terminology; it's a good investment even if you use your new knowledge only to demystify your own legal documents.

If you have word processing skills and would like to get into the law field, take a course in legal terminology as a first step. It will help tremendously on temporary assignments, no matter how simple they are, and with increased confidence and understanding you'll reach your goal much faster. If a course is not feasible and you have a lot of self-discipline, you could simply study on your own with a textbook. Such textbooks may be available at local colleges and libraries. Larger bookstores that have law sections may also sell them.

SCIENCE AND BIOTECHNOLOGY TEMPS

"I can't believe there's so much unemployment in this country when I'm inundated with calls from biotech companies screaming for people to work in their laboratories," Donald Truss, president of Science Temps in Cranford, New Jersey, told me in an interview. "Anybody who has an associate degree in a science, or possibly math, can work in a lab in an entry-level capacity. Sometimes all it takes is a really good course in chemistry or biology that includes basic laboratory skills and equipment."

"The biotechnology field is booming," said Truss. "Twenty years ago a chemist would sit on a stool and inject one sample, then read a magazine for 15 minutes while waiting for the results. Today the process is so automated that 100 samples can be injected and left overnight, and the results are all ready to read the next morning. As a result, chemists have been replaced by technicians, the industry has become much faster paced, and the opportunities for temps are unlimited."

With lab data now analyzed by computer, computer pros are in high demand. Lawyers are often called in to handle the legal details of patents for new products and contracts with pharmaceutical and other client companies. And, of course, no office or lab could run without support staff, so some science temp help companies have limited openings for entry-level personnel as well as professionals.

SCIENCE AND BIOTECHNOLOGY TEMPS

Temps needed include chemists, chemical engineers, biologists, microbiologists, environmental scientists, physicists, nuclear physicists, expert witnesses for litigation, lab technicians of all kinds, lawyers, biologists, computer specialists, pharmacists, engineers, computer pros, and office support staff.

Zach Marks, a vice president at Science Temps, has a database that includes 20,000 resumes and runs the gamut of skills, from Ph.D.'s who have spent 30 years investigating rubber failures and now testify as expert witnesses in auto accident trials, to high school graduates who wash glasses in laboratories. But most of the temps his company places have at least a bachelor's degree and two to four years of work experience.

Since science fields, particularly biotechnology, are booming and are expected to expand well into the twenty-first century, companies in these fields are promising places to find temporary work and even permanent positions.

PAY RATES

If you're good at math and science, you could rise quickly with each additional science and lab course you take. A temporary lab tech with a high school education and two years' experience or an associate degree and one year of experience can make $12 to $14 an hour. Someone with a bachelor's degree and two years' experience can make $15 to $17 an hour. And a pharmacist or Ph.D. can make $24 to $26 an hour. For an expert witness, the salary range is around $100 to $150 an hour.

GAINING WORK EXPERIENCE

Thomas R. Parham has worked as a temporary lab technician for three years through Science Temps while in premed school, getting his college degree in genetics. He started out as an entry-level lab tech and has received raises and promotions several times.

His assignments have included inspecting products, containers, and foods for quality assurance standards. "Part of the job of inspecting ice cream was to taste it once every hour, eight hours a day, to make sure the taste was correct," he told me. "I ate pints of it. I didn't have to eat that much, but I liked it," he joked.

Parham sees his experience as an important stepping-stone in his career. He knows that when he's through school he'll have little trouble finding a job, unlike other graduates who have an education but no experience. His education as a science temp has been twofold: Not only has he learned specific skills such as testing, sampling, and quality assurance inspection using state-of-the-art equipment but he's also learned operations standards and procedures in a variety of laboratories in many science fields.

One of the biggest advantages of temping, he said, is finding out what he *doesn't* want to do when he graduates. "I can't tell you how many times I've changed my major. I've met so many people in this business who sing the 'If Only Blues'—if only I'd studied this, if only I'd known about that. I hear it every day from people who end up wishing for their entire careers, which might be 40 years, that they had taken another route. Talking to people in the business every day has helped tremendously in figuring out what I want to do with my career."

COMPUTER TEMPS

It's a simple matter of fact that there are not enough skilled computer people to keep pace with industry growth. So if you have strong computer skills you should feel pretty secure about finding temporary work—as long as you keep your training current. As anyone in the industry knows, what's hot today could be outdated tomorrow.

Build a good knowledge base and then keep adding to it. Even high-tech computer pros continually take courses to keep up with advances in the computer world. No one has to tell you that we're in a global market today. Constant computer training and retraining is essential.

COMPUTER TEMPS

Temps needed include all levels of computer professionals, from entry-level to expert, such as software engineers, salespeople, tech writers, programmers, trainers, operators, word processors, graphic artists, and administrative assistants. Fields include law, science, medicine, accounting, banking, manufacturing, video, multimedia, and publishing, just to name a few.

PUBLISHING TEMPS

Publishing is a very competitive field for anyone in the business, whether they're full-time employees, freelancers, or temporaries. As a temp you must have top-notch skills and usually a degree to join the ranks, but temping can be a real door-opener once you're in a company.

"You can often move up the ranks on a temp track in publishing much faster than if a company puts you on a career track," explained Janet Christopher, vice president of operations at Advance Personnel Associates Inc., in Burlington, Massachusetts. "I saw a temporary proofreader move up to editing and then writing in two years. In a full-time job that wouldn't be as likely to happen. A temp by definition is a more mobile person, and often being in the right place at the right time pays off careerwise."

Christopher told me that ten years ago clients were willing to train temps for a day or two if they had the right background, but today specific, highly developed skills are expected. Advance Personnel relies on a computer with a database of 6,000 scanned-in resumes that will sort skills in a variety of ways to provide the client with the right temporary help.

If you do get work through a publishing temp help company and prove yourself capable, ask for advice on enhancing your background to increase your chances of getting continuous assignments.

PUBLISHING TEMPS

Temps needed include creative and technical writers, editors, graphic artists, desktop publishers, proofreaders, indexers, and high-tech publishing computer professionals.

TECHNICAL PUBLISHING TEMPS

Publishing is not limited to books and magazines; it has a high-tech side as well. Marketing materials such as computer-produced brochures and advertisements are a couple of examples; so are multimedia computer presentations incorporating animation, sound, film, and graphics.

And then there are very sophisticated computer-generated educational and training materials used in high schools, colleges, and corporate training programs. With a tap on the keyboard students can bring an entire library of information to the screen, including video, film clips, dictionaries, and pathways leading to related information. Some computerized presentations will even quiz students and grade their responses.

There's a growing market for technical publishing temps who

can work on any of these kinds of projects. They can do their work on their computers at home or in a client company's facility.

The background needed for temporary positions in these high-tech publishing areas varies, but advanced computer skills are a must; no entry-level temps need apply. Tech writers, for instance, don't necessarily need an engineering or technical background (although some engineers work as tech writers), but they do need to understand enough about engineering to write on various high-tech subjects.

The pay scale in this segment of the temporary publishing industry is very wide, ranging anywhere from $12 to $50 an hour.

ACCOUNTING AND FINANCE TEMPS

One of the biggest changes Olsten Technical Services, a division of Olsten Corporation headquartered in Westbury, New York, has seen is the increase in the number of high-level executives working as temporaries in such fields as accounting. "We had an accounting temp with us for ten years who had been chief financial officer for a Fortune 500 company; he had a bachelor's degree from Harvard and an M.B.A. from Columbia," Bob Lyons, Olsten's special services vice president, told me. "And he's only one of many high-level executives we have registered. Client companies are only beginning to realize the level of expertise available to them from the temporary help service industry."

Some of these professionals are using temporary work as a way to get inside a company in hopes of permanent placement. Others are using temp work as a way to build up their resumes and their network of potential clients for their own consulting companies.

ENVIRONMENTAL ACCOUNTING SPECIALISTS

Another interesting trend in accounting is the need for environmental accounting specialists. The increased demand for these experts is the direct result of the rapid growth in one particular area of public accounting: litigation support. The sheer number of environmental lawsuits and public policy debates has opened the door for CPA firms to take on a variety of new kinds of work: evaluating the fiscal impact of regulations, measuring the economic consequences of environmental mishaps, and determining the cost of cleanup.

ACCOUNTING AND FINANCE TEMPS

Temps needed include staff accountants, tax accountants, financial analysts, third-party billers, spreadsheet operators, payroll accountants, data entry operators, accounts payable/receivable clerks, credit and collection clerks, bookkeepers, mutual fund accountants, cost accountants, chief accountants, international tax accountants, mortgage processors, portfolio review personnel, mortgage operations personnel, origination administrators, phone reps, customer service personnel, 401(k) professionals, experts in industry-specific software, and loan processors.

CPA firms are looking for specialists who already have some experience in environmental consulting. Experts who have worked for government agencies or oil companies are in particular demand because of their familiarity with environmental regulations. Subspecialties such as business and projections, damage assessment, insurance regulations, and real estate are also highly valued.[33]

CREATIVE TEMPS

There's no business like show business. And there are no people like show people, as Deb Hester, founder and president of Chameleon Creatives, based in Tacoma, Washington, will tell you. Hester's had to deal with temps who have refused to change out of paint clothes, brush their teeth, or leave their children with a sitter before reporting for assignments. She even had one guy who would have shown up for a business meeting in punk-rock face paint if a rainstorm hadn't melted his handiwork.

Perhaps at one time "true artists" could get away with being wildly eccentric, but not today—at least if they want to eat. If you're creative and you'd like to temp in this very competitive field, you'll need up-to-date, top-notch skills as well as a willingness to conform just a little bit. "I try to advise my creatives on what services are selling and suggest where to get training," Hester told me. "If they can't keep up with the industry and have nothing else to offer, my clients can't use them and neither can I."

A good example of what Hester means is a gifted graphic designer she knows who adamantly refuses to learn computer graphics. "Unfortunately," said Hester, "in many cases it doesn't matter if you're the best designer in the client's area; the client just won't work with you if you can't do your design work on a computer."

The temp work opportunities for "creative" temps such as creative writers, actors, musicians, and graphic designers is limited, and, as you might guess, most work is found in major cities.

Temping Temptations

Lest you think that temping can only be serious business—to earn money and advance in your career—here's a look at the kind of fun and adventure you can have while you're temping, if you're so inclined. There is, after all, more to life than work. And so I leave you with some temping temptations.

TRAVEL TEMPING

Have you ever had an impulse to just take off and live someplace else for a while but couldn't because you didn't have the money and were afraid you wouldn't find a job once you got there? Maybe you want to ski in the Rockies or finally get your fill of Las Vegas, explore a desert, ride horses, see whales, visit all the national parks, learn to surf, feel the heartbeat of a major city, or end your workday with a walk on a quiet beach?

Travel temping—earning your living as a temp while exploring new places—may be a way to make your dreams come true.

U.S. TRAVEL

People have always used temporary work to move about the country. Some moved to better their prospects in what they hoped would be greener pastures and then temped while they were job shopping. Others moved because they felt like it and then, when the money ran out, found some temporary jobs to tide them over.

In the 1960s, especially, there was a certain romance in being on the road. And that romance attracted large numbers of young people, who traveled the country using temporary work to get by. Today, hitting the road is not quite as easy as it was when gas and food were cheap and vans were popular places in which to live, but people are still doing it. And some are making a real success of it.

Who's travel temping today? Young people just starting out on their own, couples who have portable skills, even seniors. And for some young retirees who can't afford to turn down attractive early retirement options yet aren't ready to give up work totally, travel temping has proved to be ideal.

Take radiologist John Gosch-Barker, M.D., for example. As he approached 60, the Navy's then-mandatory retirement age, he realized he wasn't ready to quit practicing medicine. Working on a temporary basis for CompHealth/Kron, a company that specializes in placing health care professionals, meant he didn't have to. He now works when and where he wants.[34]

You'd probably expect that highly skilled professionals would have an easy time finding assignments around the country, and they do. But what about people—perhaps like you—who don't have such skills? How can they—you—land temping assignments away from home?

If you have a good track record with a temp help company that has offices nationwide, you can ask your coordinator to fax your records ahead to your destination city so you'll already have your paperwork done and a good recommendation waiting when you get there.

There's no guarantee that you'll find all the work you need once you arrive, but you'll certainly improve your odds. I talked to several companies with offices around the country, and none had any objections to sending records on, provided they were doing it for someone they could recommend. To make the grade you must have scored well on any tests, received good reviews from client companies, and worked with the temp help company long enough that your coordinator knows and trusts you.

Other ways to plan ahead include:

- calling temp help companies in your destination city to find out what the job prospects are for people with your skills
- sending for the yellow pages from your destination city to check out temp help companies' listings and display ads
- getting current local newspapers from your destination city and looking at employment and temp help ads in the classified sections
- asking for an interview with one of the larger temp help companies that has computerized national databases of both temp employees and clients. These companies can often match skills with out-of-state assignments; that's what the database is for. Tell them where you're going, if you know, or where you'd like to go if there's temp work available there.

OVERSEAS TRAVEL

The more in demand your skills are, the further they can take you—literally. To travel overseas you've got to speak the language and have very specific expertise foreign companies can't find enough of at home. Some health professionals find temp work in countries where there is a shortage of medical expertise. Engineers and other highly skilled technical temps with specialized knowledge can also find work.

Most American temp help companies don't arrange work for U.S. temps in foreign countries; it's too difficult for recruiters here to handle the work permits and all the other red tape involved. If you have advanced expertise and want to temp abroad, contact one of the larger temp help companies that has offices overseas; it can put you in touch with branches there.

LOCUM TENENS TRAVELERS

Japan, Australia, Mexico, France, Saudi Arabia, Egypt, Qatar, Mexico . . . this is just a sampling of the countries you can work in if you have excellent skills in medical fields. It's estimated that 10,000 doctors and even larger numbers of nurses are traveling the world today, administering needed medical care while seeing the U.S. and sometimes the world.

Also traveling these days, at least in the U.S., are psychiatrists, psychologists, allergists, respiratory therapists, anesthesiologists, nurse anesthesiologists, dermatologists, certified nurse midwives, physical therapists, medical technologists, radiologic technologists, physician assistants, speech and language pathologists, and occupational therapists.

It would be hard to turn down some of the offers made by companies that specialize in placing traveling health care professionals. Not only do health professionals who travel often make more money per hour; in some cases their travel expenses are paid for, all the work arrangements are taken care of, a furnished apartment awaits them, medical insurance is paid for, and bonuses of up to $1,000 may be available just for completing the assignment.

A TRAVELING NURSE

Lisa Noe is a medical/surgical nurse who has been traveling with TravCorps, headquartered in Malden, Massachusetts, for three years now. For each three-month assignment she takes she is provided with a furnished apartment, free transportation, and free health, life, and dental services, not to mention cash bonuses.

"When I started," she told me, "I meant to take only one assignment. But now that it's in my blood I can't seem to get it out. I've been all over the country and to Hawaii twice. I really enjoy the lifestyle. You don't really get to know an area until you live there, and I've lived all over the country."

Far from being lonely on the road, Lisa said she socializes more when she's traveling than when she's at home. "When you're on an assignment in a new place," she said, "you're always going out to visit places you've never seen before, and you're with other travelers who want to do the same things. At this point, my best friends are travelers; I send Christmas cards to London, St. Thomas, Hawaii, the Bahamas. And I have a friend I usually travel with and often room with. We even ask for the same weekends off so we can explore together."

Hospital assignments are usually for three months, which, Lisa says, "is long enough to make friends but not long enough to get involved in the hospital politics or get too homesick." When she's home and between assignments, Lisa works in a hospital in-house per diem pool.

A TRAVELING DOCTOR

One doctor I interviewed, Mark Stevenson, who specializes in family practice medicine, told me that after years in medical school and then residency he wanted to travel for a while and explore his work options before settling on a location and establishing his practice.

In two and a half years as a locum tenens doctor, he's had a variety of jobs. He has been the ship's doctor for 900 crew members and 2,500 passengers on cruise ships in the Caribbean; he's worked in remote areas of Hawaii, including a sugar plantation village of 2,900; and he's treated people in Colorado ski resorts. Most of his assignments were arranged by CompHealth/Kron, based in Salt Lake City, Utah, but he's also been an independent contractor, arranging his own assignments with health-care facilities.

When I caught up with him, he was working in Yellowstone National Park, filling in for vacationing physicians—an arrangement he set up himself. About half the patients he was seeing were tourists, and the other half were area residents. "It's great here," he said. "I backpack during my time off, and I've seen a lot of the park I'd never have seen as a tourist—you could spend years seeing this place. I've never had a bad experience as a locum tenens physician, but then I check the assignment out by talking to staff physicians before I accept it."

Mark has had opportunities to work in big cities, small towns, hospitals, clinics, health maintenance organizations (HMOs), and private offices, which he feels has added much to his experiences as a physician.

In addition to having the opportunity to "try out" different types of medicine and medical settings, Mark also enjoys a lot of time off (he works ten months out of the year) and works when and where he wants. If he doesn't like the assignments offered, he can wait for one he does want. Another benefit is money. Mark says he could probably make more in his own practice but reasons that he has more disposable income than physicians who practice on their own or in a group. Although he does have to pay for his own health insurance and receives no retirement benefits, he has no living expenses. He paid off $25,000 in student loans during his first year of practice.

Will he ever give up locum tenens work? "Probably," he told me. "But I met one guy who's worked as a locum tenens physician for 15 years, working—by choice—only eight months out of the year."

VACATION TEMPING

Hopping on a plane every few months and flying for as long as 24 hours at a time (in the case of overseas travel) isn't for everyone. Neither is constantly packing and unpacking and never being "settled." For people with families, houses, and pets, travel temping can be close to impossible. An alternative is to do what some people call "vacation temping."

Dr. John Gosch-Barker, the retired navy radiologist introduced earlier in this section, said he and his wife have a 150-year-old house they're restoring in Newport, Rhode Island, and two kids in college. When he's travel temping around the country to earn money for his children's tuition and for construction supplies, he lives in a motor home with his wife, their cats, and a parrot for two- to four-week stints. "It gets a little noisy sometimes," Gosch-Barker said, "but I like to travel."[35]

Lou Green, a retired engineer from New England, partially paid for his family's last two winters in Orlando, Florida, by picking up temporary engineering assignments. "I had a hard time with retirement," he said. "I had always been so absorbed in my work and then

. . . nothing. Golf's okay for a while, but I've never been obsessive about it. Temping keeps me busy and brings in extra money.

"I take a temporary assignment, work on a project until it's completed, and then I'm off for as long as I want. It's been good for my family. When we go to Florida, we rent a good-size house or condo so the kids and grandkids can come down for visits. If it weren't for temporary work, I don't think we could keep our house plus spend the winter in Florida. This way, we have the best of both worlds."

TAKING A BREAK FROM THE RAT RACE

When you're between jobs in your field, it's wise to pursue temporary jobs that can open doors for you, but you might want to keep your eyes open for opportunities that can be good for your mental health too.

Wouldn't you occasionally like to get away from your own field, where you always have to perform, and try something new? As a temporary worker you have lots of opportunities to take a break from the mainstream world and float away on a tributary just for a little while.

As a temporary you're your own boss. You're free. There's no law that says you have to take work in your field when you can make the same money in a different field and have more fun and fewer headaches once in a while. Let your coordinator know you're game for anything as long as you get your current rate. Then see what turns up.

FAR AWAY FROM AN OFFICE

As a temp out in the country, even if you sign on to be an office worker of some type, you could be offered a day's work as a bale tosser, corn detassler, grape picker . . . the list goes on. I heard of one woman in Colorado who got a week's assignment on a farm as a goat milker because she included her cow-milking experience on her application for temporary work and someone actually called the temp help company looking for someone with milking skills!

I don't know about you, but there are lots of times when I'd much prefer being outside in a corn field on a glorious summer's day than stuck inside a stuffy office. In fact, even though I live only an hour's drive from Boston, which isn't exactly America's breadbasket, I did spend a few days as a farm hand for Farmer Dan (that's what he calls himself) and loved every minute of it. I don't claim it wasn't hard work—it was—but it was such a refreshing change from office work that I wish I'd had more opportunities like it.

And I'll never forget the spring I spent barefoot in shorts and a T-shirt on a seasonal job sanding and painting sailboats in a tiny New England harbor. It was one of my favorite work experiences. I still feel peaceful when I remember the sun on the water and the creaking of the boat as it rocked idly beneath me.

Most people may find it hard to believe that sanding and painting anything could be fun, but for me, after working far too many hours at a high-stress job, sitting cross-legged on a warm deck with a cool ocean breeze at my back and only gulls for company was heaven, in spite of the paint fumes and paint chips in my eyes.

I found the experience much more relaxing than a vacation. When I was on vacation, my job was always in the back of my mind; I could never really forget it. But that particular spring, I gave myself permission to relax. Why not? I was making better money than I had been in my previous office work, and I knew I could temp again whenever I needed to. I also knew that if I enjoyed this "time out" I would be better equipped to deal with my high-stress career once I got back into it.

And I was right. I did take another full-time job. But during those few months working on boats, I came and went as I pleased. As a bonus, I got lots of invitations to go sailing. When it rained, I took temporary jobs. (This is one time when I asked for very short-term assignments, lasting only a few days at most.)

TEMPING FOR FUN

Ever wonder what it'd be like to play Santa Claus (and get paid for it)? Where do you think those jolly St. Nicks you see at department stores, shopping malls, and holiday parties and events come from? Did you know that some temp help companies actually have

Santa divisions? The pay's about $6 an hour, and the laughs are free. You can also be the Easter Bunny, a Smurf, or Abe Lincoln, depending on the season and the setting.

MUSICAL MADNESS

Sometimes you don't even have to look for fun assignments—they're offered to you. I remember one assignment in particular where I earned great money, had flexible hours, and was so relaxed I wasn't sure I was working.

Before the proofreader of a major celebrity magazine went on what she called "a badly needed vacation," she filled me in on what needed to be done. As she talked, I looked around the office, which was a converted sail loft overlooking the ocean. To say everyone was dressed casually would be the understatement of the year. I felt overdressed without holes in my jeans. Signed photos of popular musicians covered one wall, and the very latest in rock music was blasting (and I mean blasting) over two huge speakers.

"Here's a story for you to proofread," the employee said. "And you'll be getting a few more as the deadline gets closer." Just a glance told me I was looking at an interview with one of the most famous rock stars of all time. For someone who had spent a year proofreading an oil industry magazine featuring articles on subjects like mud, this hardly seemed like work.

"I heard it's juicy—lots of gossip and name-dropping," the proofreader told me. "You might want to use the soundproof room, though. The writers are reviewing new albums, and it can get crazy in here when they like them." She rolled her eyes in obvious annoyance. "They keep wanting you to dance with them."

Before she left, she told me there were cans of beer in the soft drink machine. And—I swear—her parting words were "I hope it doesn't get too tedious for you."

Some jobs are clearly better than others.

FOLLOW YOUR DREAMS

What are your dreams? Do you want to write, paint, dance, act, sail, model, go to college, run marathons, climb mountains?

Maybe you could live out your dream if you knew you had temporary work as a backup.

As I've said elsewhere, I would never encourage anyone to quit a full-time job to take temporary work unless money and benefits are not an issue. Even then, you should do it only after you've researched your temp opportunities carefully enough to know that temping is really a viable option for you.

Once you have proved to yourself that you can get temp work and know it's there to fall back on, you won't be so hesitant about exploring possibilities and going after what you really want. It may mean scrambling, depending on your skills, but if you're determined to live by your dreams it can be done.

I know a now-successful male model who used to supplement his modeling work with temporary light industrial work so that he could be available when a modeling assignment came up. I also know an artist who quit her job in a laboratory to paint and now temps in labs when she needs to supplement her income from her art sales. And I suspect most of us know people who would much prefer to work really hard most of the year to pay for a long vacation they can take when they want to.

What jobs would you really love to take if only you could afford to? Do you love boating? You could try out a job on a windjammer, cruise ship, or river boat. Have you ever wanted to be a roadie for a band or work on a movie set or in a summer camp or resort? Do you want to try teaching tennis, golf, scuba diving, or a foreign language for a while?

People work all of these jobs, and they're not necessarily young. The pay may be low, the security zilch, and the work short-term, but they accept all the risks for the experience and personal satisfaction they get in return. If you have proved to yourself that you can depend on temporary work to get you through slow times or keep you going when your personal adventure is over, you, too, can follow your dreams.

A Glossary of Temporary Help Terms

Agency: An employment agency.

Applicant: An individual seeking temporary employment with a temporary help company. In employment agencies, an applicant is a person seeking permanent placement.

Assign: To send a temporary employee to work on the premises of a customer of the temporary help company. *Assign* differs from *refer,* which describes the employment agency practice of sending an applicant to a prospective employer for an interview. *Refer* and *referral* do not apply to assigning temporary employees.

Assignment: The period during which a temporary employee is working on a customer's premises.

Client company: The company temps are sent to by the temporary help company they work for.

Client contact: The person at the client company who will greet temps on the first day of an assignment and introduce them to the people they'll be working for. Often this person works in the human resources department and has arranged the details and conditions of the assignment with the coordinator of the temp help company.

Contingent work force: The approximately 32 million workers— part-timers, temps, and independent contractors—who do not work full time but instead work contingent to the needs of business. An estimated 1.2 million people currently work as temps; 9.5 million as independent contractors; 15 million as voluntary part-time workers; and 6.5 million as involuntary part-time workers (people who would be working full time if they could but have been laid off or had their hours reduced).

Coordinator: The staff employee of a temporary help company who assigns temporary employees to work on the customer's premises.

Counselor: An employment agency employee who refers or places applicants with employers. The term does not apply to a staff employee of a temporary help company.

Customer: The person, organization, or business that uses the services of a temporary help company.

Dispatch: To assign industrial temporary employees to report for work on customers' premises.

Downsizing: The business trend toward scaling down the number of employees to a minimum of essential workers, often supplemented, as needed, by contingent workers.

Employee leasing: An arrangement in which a business transfers its employees to the payroll of a leasing organization, after which the employees are leased back to their original employer, where they work in the same capacity as before in an ongoing, permanent relationship.

Employment agency: A business that brings a job seeker and a prospective employer together in a permanent relationship.

Executive temps: High-level executives, such as CEOs, who are working on a temporary basis.

Facilities management: Sometimes referred to as managed services or simply outsourcing, this is a service provided by an organization that supplies both staff and management to perform a specific client function or functions on an ongoing, indefinite basis. The service provider is not only responsible for supplying and supervising the staff but also has overall management accountability for results, output, etc. Examples include operating a mail room or data processing center or supplying cafeteria services, guard services, or maintenance and janitorial services.

Facilities staffing: A service provided by an organization that supplies staff to perform a specific client function or functions on an ongoing, indefinite basis. The service provider may offer coordination or supervision of staff, but unlike facilities management does not have overall management accountability for results, output, etc.

Fee: The amount charged by an employment agency for placing job seekers in permanent positions. The term does not refer to a temporary help company's gross profit or liquidated damages charge.

General employer: An employer who has the right to hire and fire an employee, is responsible for the employee's wages and benefits, and exercises ultimate supervision, discipline, and control over the employee. Temporary help companies are the general employers of their temporary employees.

In-house temporary: An individual hired directly by a company other than a temporary help company as a permanent employee to perform various assignments.

Independent contractor: A person who is not an employee who performs work for another. Unlike employees, independent contractors are not subject to the control and supervision of the person using the services regarding the details of how the work is to be performed; generally have specialized training or education; and supply all tools, supplies, or equipment necessary to perform the work.

Job shop: A colloquial term generally used to refer to temp help companies that supply longer-term temporary employees on a contract basis in technical or specialized areas.

Joint operations: The operation of both a temporary help company and an employment agency by the same firm. Problems arise when these fundamentally different operations are run with the same personnel, forms, and procedures (commingling) so that it's difficult for job applicants and customers to distinguish between the two businesses.

Just-in-time staffing: The practice of using a flexible staff of contingent workers to supplement a company's traditional work force as needed in response to production demands.

Liquidated damages: Monies paid by temporary help customers under contracts in which the customer agrees not to hire the temporary employee within some specified period and to pay damages for breach of that promise in the agreed-upon amount.

Locum tenens: The term used for temporary doctors and other health professionals, many of whom travel across the country and sometimes throughout the world on assignment. Literally the term means "one holding a place."

Niche temp help company: A company that concentrates on an area or areas of expertise in a specialized industry. A temp help company that specializes in placing experts in a particular language would be an example.

Part time: A work period less than the full workday or full workweek. Part-time employees differ from temporary employees because they work a regular schedule for their employer on an ongoing, indefinite basis.

Payrolling: In one form of payrolling, a customer, rather than the temporary help company, recruits an individual and asks the temporary help company to consider employing the individual and assigning him to the customer on a temporary basis. This may occur when the client has a specialized need and is in the best position to screen applicants for the required skills.

Another form of payrolling involves current employees of the customer whom the customer transfers to the payroll of the staffing firm. For example, an employee near retirement who is engaged in a project expected to continue beyond his scheduled retirement date can be "payrolled" with a staffing firm until the project is completed without disrupting his normal retirement schedule.

Per diem: The payment terms most often used for temp work in health and human services fields. Per diem workers are paid by the day or by the assignment.

Placement: An employment agency term for placing a job seeker in a permanent position with an employer.

Pretrained temps: Temps who are trained to fulfill client companies' specific needs before they are sent on an assignment. Data entry operators, for instance, are now being trained to use client companies' forms and equipment before they begin working on-site. Pretrained temps are also becoming available in banking, insurance, manufacturing, and electronics industries.

Right sizing: Operating with a core of full-time employees, often supplemented with contingent workers as needed.

Special employer: Refers to a customer's legal relationship to the temporary employees assigned to that customer, based on the customer's right to direct and control the specific details of the work to be performed. As special employers, customers have certain legal rights and obligations regarding temporary employees. For example, because workers' compensation insurance (which temporary help companies provide for their employees) is the exclusive relief available to employees against employers for work-related injuries, a temporary employee generally cannot sue his special employer (the customer) for negligence.

Specialized temp help company: A company that specializes in one particular industry, such as computers, engineering, law, medicine, or science.

Supplemental staffing: The practice of supplementing the permanent staff of hospitals and nursing homes with nurses and other health care personnel employed by temporary help companies.

Temporary employee: An employee who does not make a commitment to an employer to work on a regular, ongoing basis but is free to accept or reject assignments as he or she chooses. A temporary employer furnishes its own employees (known as temporaries) to satisfy customers' temporary staffing needs and special projects.

Temporary help service: A service that supplies its own employees to support or supplement a client's work force in special work situations such as employee absences, temporary skill shortages, seasonal or peak workloads, and special assignments and projects.

Temp-to-permanent: Also referred to as "try before you hire," it's the practice of sending temporary employees on an assignment for the express purpose of ultimately placing them in a permanent position with the company.

Work order: An order received from a customer for a temporary help company's services.

Most of the terms in this glossary are based on the National Association of Temporary Services' "Lexicon of Terms." Reprinted with permission of the National Association of Temporary Services, 119 South Asaph Street, Alexandria, Virginia 22314.

Useful Publications and Organizations

Executive Recruiter News publishes a *Directory of Temporary Firms,* available for $19 from Kennedy Publications, Templeton Rd., Fitzwilliam, NH 03447; 603-585-6544; 800-531-0007.

You may also look into the following publications for further information on temporary work, although the target audience may be companies seeking or placing temporary help rather than temporary workers.

Guide to Locum Tenens Recruitment, American Medical Association; 800-621-8335 (ask for OP #392292). About $20 for non-AMA members.

Tempdigest, 10500 Forum Place Drive, Suite 420, Houston, TX 77036; 800-444-0674. A magazine published for the temporary service industry.

Cooperative Concepts, Susan Minzter, 948 Wyandotte Trail, Westfield, NJ 07090; 908-654-1195. A training and development consulting company that conducts workshops for temporary workers who want to discover how temping can work for them, understand the temporary market, and make the most from temping.

National Association of Temporary Services, 119 South Saint Asaph St., Alexandria, VA 22314; 703-549-6287. Provides legal, legislative, regulatory, and industry-related activities and information on behalf of its temporary help service members.

Notes

1. Michael R. Losey, "Temps: They're Not Just for Typing Anymore," *Modern Office Technology,* August 1991, p. 5.
2. "Profile of a Typical Temporary Employee," reprinted from *Contemporary Times,* Winter 1989, National Association of Temporary Services. Study conducted by Lauer, Lalley and Associates, Inc., Washington, D.C.
3. "Temporary Employment Can Lead to Better Pay and Jobs," press release, National Association of Temporary Services, March 11, 1992.
4. *Ibid.*
5. "Profile of a Typical Temporary Employee," reprinted from *Contemporary Times,* Winter 1989, National Association of Temporary Services. Study conducted by Lauer, Lalley and Associates, Inc., Washington, D.C.
6. *ERN Special Report,* a newsletter published by *Executive Recruiter News,* October 1991, Section 1, p. 1.
7. *ERN Special Report,* a newsletter published by *Executive Recruiter News,* October 1991, Section 1, p. 2.
8. "Profile of a Typical Temporary Employee," reprinted from *Contemporary Times,* Winter 1989, National Association of Temporary Services. Study conducted by Lauer, Lalley and Associates, Inc., Washington, D.C.
9. Jeff Donn, "Next Assignment: Find a Job," Associated Press, reprinted in the *Boston Globe,* May 1992, p. 16.
10. Paige Kester-Beaver, "Tales From Travelers," *American*

Journal of Nursing, Vol. 91, No. 4, April 1991, pp. 50-56. Copyright 1991, American Journal of Nursing Company.

11. *Make More of Your Retirement,* National Association of Temporary Services brochure.

12. *ERN Special Report,* a newsletter published by *Executive Recruiter News,* October 1991, p. 3.

13. *ERN Special Report,* a newsletter published by *Executive Recruiter News,* October 1991, p. 5.

14. Ernest R. Sander, "Life in the Temp Lane," *Boston Phoenix,* Section Two, Oct. 23, 1992, pp. 6-7.

15. Patricia S. Fuller, "Temping," *Tempdigest,* Vol. 6, No. 1, Fall 1989, p. 38.

16. Michael R. Losey, "Temps: They're Not Just for Typing Anymore," *Modern Office Technology,* August 1991, p. 5.

17. Patricia S. Fuller, "Temping," *Tempdigest,* Vol. 6, No. 1, Fall 1989, p. 38.

18. Nancy O'Brien, "Orientation of a New Temp," *The Best of Tempdigest—The First Five Years,* pp. 111-14. Copyright 1989 by Tempdigest International, Inc.

19. Mary E. Willard, "A 'Road Map' for Working Temp," *Tempdigest,* Vol. 6, No. 1, Fall 1989, p. 28.

20. Nancy O'Brien, "Orientation of a New Temp," *The Best of Tempdigest—The First Five Years,* pp. 111-14. Copyright 1989 by Tempdigest International.

21. *Ibid.*

22. Bernice Kanner, "Bernice Kanner Pays Her Dues as a Temp," *New York,* April 2, 1990, pp. 41-44.

23. Susan M. Minzter, "Twelve Tips for Temps," excerpted from *Making Temping Work for You* (Westfield, NJ: Cooperative Concepts, 1989).

24. Susan McHenry and Linda Lee Small, "Does Part-Time Pay Off?," *Ms.,* March 1989, pp. 88-94.

25. "Retooling the Office Work Force," *The Office Professional* (a newsletter published by Professional Training Associates, Inc.), Vol. 10, No. 1, Jan. 15, 1990.

26. "Temp Agency Offers Benefits," *Boston Globe,* March 9, 1993, p. 39.

27. Amy Norton Paterson, "To Specialize or Not to Specialize? That Is the Question," *Tempdigest,* Vol. 8, No. 1, Fall 1991, p. 50.

28. "The 25 Hottest Careers," *Working Woman,* July 1993, pp. 41-51.

29. *ERN Special Report,* a newsletter published by *Executive Recruiter News,* September 1992, p. 2.

30. Susan Diesenhouse, "In a Shaky Economy, Even Professionals Are Temps," *New York Times,* May 16, 1993, p. 5.

31. Dyan Machan, "Rent-an-exec," *Forbes,* Jan. 22, 1990, pp. 132-33.

32. Barbara Bernardo, *Paralegal* (Princeton, NJ: Peterson's, 1993), p. 124.

33. "Environmental Disasters Creating New Breed of Accountants," *Tempdigest,* Vol. 9, No. 1, Fall 1992, p. 20.

34. "Delivering doctors on demand—Temp work fills gaps, provides career options for physicians," *USA Today,* April 7, 1992. Reprinted with permission by CompHealth for brochure insert.

35. *Ibid.*

Index